A GLANCE TOWARD SHAKESPEARE

A GLANCE TOWARD SHAKESPEARE

BY

JOHN JAY CHAPMAN

ATLANTIC MONTHLY PRESS
BOSTON

Printed in United States of America

CONTENTS

APPENDIX

A GLANCE TOWARD SHAKESPEARE

I

INTRODUCTION

THE use of great men is to bind the world together. Everybody knows of them, thinks and writes about them, till they become portions of the common mind. An aftercomer cannot tell his own story, or even see life clearly, without reference to those who have controlled the world's thought in the past. And thus the names of great men become a part of the elemental power of language itself. Shakespeare's works touch our life and mind at all points, and he is himself behind most of our critical perceptions. He illumines our atmosphere, and the prismatic lights and shadows that he casts through each generation are moving and transitory things. I have, therefore, not ventured to call the papers by a title more ambitious than a glance toward the light.

It was near the end of the eighteenth century that men began to realize the greatness of Shakespeare, and literary persons were then visited with a new, vague, and strange experience — the discovery that the power of Shakespeare was beyond the reach of criticism. The labors of scholarship over the poet have spread the news, till it has become a commonplace. One finds in the classics, whether of Greek or

Roman times, much reverence for critical theory. At Athens and at Rome all parties had a religious belief in the power of criticism. This breaking of shackles, this plunging of the mind into a mystery that shines the more because it defies analysis, is Shakespeare's gift to the world.

His fame as a poet has all but eclipsed his fame as a dramatist; because poetry is a circulating medium which floats into our houses, whereas a drama implies a journey to the playhouse. It will be seen that I began these studies by a paper on the plays as poetry, for it is as poetry that Shakespeare first approaches most of us. Nevertheless, the drama, and the bones of dramatic construction, the management of plot, the arts of speech and rhetoric, are always at play in him. They are the wings of his vehicle. And thus the actual stage becomes the true place to study him. The footlights are our best guide to him; and if he should be lost to the living stage, a great part of his meaning would vanish. It is for this reason that the reader will find in these Notes various discussions of the plays as mere shows, as popular amusements, and much scattered talk about acting, enunciation, and even about children's performances.

II

THE PLAYS AS POETRY

It is strange to think that the greatest and most enduring things in literature have been written for festivals and holiday amusements, or as the pastimes of leisure. Of this nature were the Greek dramas and the earliest epic poems; of this nature were the mediæval romances, Molière's plays, Calderon's plays — whatever is greatest in drama, whatever is most eternal in fiction. To the author and to their first public, Shakespeare's plays were like street concerts, or tales told by a professional traveler. They formed a part of the current fiction of the day, and were supposed to be almost as ephemeral as charades.

Yet the greatness of Shakespeare is bound up with this fleeting and transient purpose of his plays. Their unique quality — the sense they give us of something that has never been touched by man, but has blossomed spontaneously out of the spirit — is due, in part, to the light estimate in which the stage was held in Elizabeth's time. This is what set Shakespeare free: he could give rein to his imagination, and his imagination got such mastery over him and burned so brightly, that it obscured the fuel. He had no court and no critics to please, but only the curiosity of an excitable, popular, clamorous audience, for whom he improvised a stage that obeyed no laws except the laws of his own mind and heart. The form and substance of his work is one. We know of

Shakespeare nothing but his mind. His function was to enchant men: for an hour or two, as all believed in his own day, and for many centuries, as it proved in the outcome. The charm is everywhere in him — in a phrase, in a speech, in a climax, or in the mood that lies behind them all. His wit, humor, and unexpected leaps and plunges of thought are held together by a thread of narrative which is never broken, but which tugs at us and focuses our attention on the action. The thread of the story is often the only dramatic unity to be found in a play of Shakespeare.

Whatever playwrights may claim or scholars propound, the mass of mankind reads for recreation, and it is as an engaging writer of fiction that Shakespeare has made his way. The taste for stories is eternal. In the Homeric Age the tales were recited by a bard; in the Middle Age, by a *jongleur* in a castle yard. In Elizabeth's day they were sung by ballad-mongers, until the primitive stage caught them up, and a new generation of poets turned the tales of the world into dramas. The passion behind all this popular literature, from Homer to Kipling, is a passion for fiction. The form changes from poetry to prose and back again, the subjects vary with the taste of the times; but the inner meaning and inner value of all these forms of literature is the same at all epochs — it is recreation through fiction.

Shakespeare has held his place in the world through competition with subsequent fiction. His stories are so vividly told, that even people who dislike plays and who do not care for poetry delight in them. As a rule, plays make hard reading, and it bothers us to visualize the characters. But Shakespeare's plays visualize themselves. Each character is, as it were, costumed in his own language. Erase the names of the speakers, and the text itself keeps them in place. Destroy stage directions, remove the stage from under their feet, and pull down the theatre, and yet the play goes forward: everything is expressed in the lines themselves. Every shade of emotion that flits through the heart of a character is reduced to a thought; and thus the rapidly moving story is accompanied by a cloud or nimbus of running commentary, gay or gloomy, poetic or worldly-wise according to circumstance, but always metaphysical, always Shakespeare.

These side-lights and explanations in Shakespeare are really the remarks of the narrator himself, but he has so colored them to suit each character and so woven them into the action, that they pass as mere gestures and do not dog the story too closely. They expound it, illuminate it, keep it alive. When the average man reads one of the plays for the first time, he wants to know what is going to happen. When he has satisfied this curiosity he becomes ensnared in the wit, wisdom, and beauty of the piece. He no longer cares whether the thing be a story or not; for after listening for two hours to the most inspired talker the world has ever known, almost anyone is apt to come back to his elbow. He returns to refathom the piece, for fear he may have missed something; and after this he browses in all the plays during his leisure hours, and finds pictures of low life, pictures of high life, mad, passionate romance, caustic wit, village drollery, dungeons, fairies, Roman history, English kings, many familiar words and thoughts whose origin he had not known, fragments of his own mind as it were, anticipations of his own experience, things so well said and so naturally said that he is astonished. The page vanishes, the book drops from his hand, and he is in a brown study.

Dreamy and emotional people like the plays for their poetry; humdrum people like them for their common sense. While Shakespeare was one of the most extravagant thinkers that ever lived, — a moody, brooding romanticist, — he was also a practical man, inordinately sociable, observant, and proverbial. Thus, almost anyone who has lived an active life and knows the world finds a friend in Shakespeare.

About eighty years ago there was a certain substantial merchant of Boston who retired from business with a competency, and found himself with time on his hands. A friend advised him to read Shakespeare, which he did, and was immensely impressed. "That 's a great book, sir, an extraordinary book! Why, sir, there are not ten men in Boston who could have written it!"

It would be hard to draw up a summary of Shakespeare's disciples. The "Tempest" seems to a child to be a fairy tale; but to the German scholar it is an apocalypse of certain Teutonic philosophic ideas, which are difficult for the outsider to appreciate. Ought one to begrudge his mental pasture to the German, or can we assign limits to the meanings of poetry? The plays are concentric, gyrating spheres of interest. The wit is everywhere, and draws in one man; the humor is everywhere, and draws in the next.

The perfection of utterance hypnotizes a very large class, of which I confess myself one: I forget everything in the language. The mere contrast of characters is enough to intoxicate other readers, quite apart from what the creatures do or say, somewhat as the mere coloring of the great masters excites certain beholders. One feels that these contrasts have been imagined in a region of thought that is inaccessible to the ordinary mind.

Not long ago I read "Cymbeline" aloud to a little girl of eight. It took several days, for I read every scene; and I was, of course, obliged to expound and digress from time to time, in order to make the story clear; for the plot is extremely complex and long drawn out. I am not myself very fond of "Cymbeline." It is a tissue of inordinate romantic fancy, like an enormous tapestry, for which I have no room in my house. But to the little girl it was as real as Red Riding Hood and much more thrilling. Romance rushed from the play in the fourth line of its opening, and found Imogen in the heart of the child.

SEC. GENT. But what 's the matter?
FIRST GENT. His daughter, the heir of 's kingdom, whom
He purposed to his wife's sole son — a widow
That late he married — hath referred herself
Unto a poor but worthy gentleman: she 's wedded;
Her husband banished; she imprisoned: all
Is outward sorrow; though I think the King
Be touched at very heart.

"Cymbeline" is one of Shakespeare's latest plays, and is said to be a masterpiece of dramatic virtuosity. Its poetic merits belong to those supersensuous, ecstatic, virginal enthusiasms which no one but Shakespeare has ever expressed. The play was one of Tennyson's favorites; and a copy of it was found in his hands on his deathbed and was buried with him. Here we have the child and Tennyson and certain dramatic critics all in accord over something which is — or was — but dimly visible to me.

I have read learned essays upon Shakespeare's habit of juggling with our sense of time, now seeming to accelerate, now to retard the progress of the plot, and always feeding the action with new fires. "Othello," for instance, is thought to show traces of an elaborate and calculated system of hints by which we are led to believe at one moment that some weeks have elapsed, and at the next that only an hour or two has passed, between one scene and the next. I am half afraid to examine such questions, lest the charm of the play should vanish in them; for I am convinced that such things were woven unconsciously into the marvelous fabric as it grew, and should be accepted and consumed by the reader in a passing glance, which is as unconscious as was the feeling that created them. Woe be to the man who cries "*Stand and deliver*" to Shakespeare's fancy or to life itself! While immersed in the living stream and volume of his mind, we get our share of him, and that is enough. His spectres rise in the fumes of the brain and cannot be conjured to submission. They will not seed or plough for us. They are not exactly human beings, but thoughts — phantoms that pass and repass through the castle walls of life, sit on the battlements in the sunlight, and behold, nothing is there! The tragedies and the comedies live in the same region, exciting thought, wonder, joy, surprise, admiration, but never grief. Even Ophelia does not excite grief.

> Thought, affliction, passion, hell itself,
> She turns to favor and to prettiness.

Nor King Lear, who turns sufferings to a pathos that is beyond the reach of tears. Breathless we watch them, not sorrow-stricken, not saddened, but awed; and the bright troops, motley characters, irresponsible humorists, Dogberrys, gravediggers, jailors, who flock so close to the cortège of Shakespeare's funerals, please, relieve, and console us because they too are phantoms made of the same light — deflections, pendants, the half-expected completions of a dream.

Shall we call it the Tragic or the Comic in Shakespeare that so moves us? One of Plato's most profound surmises, namely, that the genius for Tragedy and the genius for Comedy were akin, waited eighteen hundred years to be exemplified; for Shakespeare's plays show that the Tragic and the Comic are one. This remarkable idea may have occurred to Plato because he was himself a species of dramatist — an entertainer and a *jongleur;* and perhaps he happened on the idea as a trade-secret: he found it at the bottom of his pack. Tragedy and Comedy are recreations; but it was not till Shakespeare came and gave to both of them unimagined depths of meaning and of perfection that the identity of their genius was clearly revealed.

One cannot define pleasure, or name the difference between imaginative literature and realism; but it is easy to tell them apart. Imaginative work leaves us happy. But Ibsen and Tolstoy, and the modern heavy hewers of fiction, by whatever name they may call themselves, cloy the mind. Your true artist leaves behind an exhilaration and not a problem. He gives us brain-spun realities which have no function except to be apprehended by the brain. Such things on the stage will prove to be either comedy or tragedy; and sometimes they can be taken as either one or the other, according to one's mood. Many scenes throughout Shakespeare are both comic or tragic, as one may choose to think. In the "Merchant of Venice" the baffled rage of Shylock was staged as low comedy for a hundred and fifty years, till someone found out that the warp and woof of tragedy was in it. In "King Lear" Shakespeare has, here and there, mingled the two elements in one dialogue, in one conception, in one flash. The scheme of thought that runs behind his work is deeper than either tragedy or comedy. They are but parts of the masque that is danced in the foreground. The power that moves them lies behind and underneath the action.

III

ON THE STAGE

THE plays have come down to us, and have held the boards for three hundred years, throughout all the changes in social life and stage usage. Their plots and characters live in the public mind as the Greek myths lived in the mind of a Greek audience; and half the playwright's work is thus done before the curtain rises. When first staged, they were hardly divided into scenes; but consisted of a mere stream of personages, costumed sufficiently to distinguish them from one another, mounted on a primitive staging in a small theatre, who recited their lines at a rate not very different from the pace of ordinary conversation. There was little to distract the mind of the audience from the text.

The whole Elizabethan drama shows plainly enough that the age was an age of naturalism tinctured by a passion for rant and bombast. It was a furious, riotous, tatterdemalion kind of drama, and the extreme length of many of the plays proves the rapidity with which the scenes must have followed one another. The Elizabethan theatre was a mill for grinding out stories, tales, adventures, historical incidents, novels, and romances. The plot and its outcome were what the audience cared for; not problems, not tableaux, not spectacles. Such things occur, to be sure, but they seem to be dragged along sideways in the rush of the story. The public was so fond of stories that it would go to see boys act grown-up plays; not in the least because the audiences wished to encourage the drama or cared a farthing about the boys, but because of the excitement of the plots. No one to-day, except a student, would go twice to a veritable Shakespeare performance, if such a thing were possible. The chances are that we should find the old pronunciation hard to follow, and the place would seem to us like bedlam.

The plays have come down to us with a good deal of baggage which did n't belong to them originally, but which we cannot throw away *en masse*. The right staging of Shakespeare is a question of edging away from practices, whether ancient or modern, which obscure the effectiveness of the text. All the different devices that have been assembled must dissolve and disappear in the performance, showing not the stage, but the drama as it unrolled, not on a stage but in the mind of Shakespeare, who has given the best example to the rest of the troupe by disappearing himself.

That Shakespeare is overloaded with thought is indubitable, yet the very plays which are most overloaded with thought are the ones where the action moves most rapidly. The "Tempest," "King Lear," "Macbeth," the "Merchant of Venice" hold the public to-day by their pristine appeal as stories. They hold it in spite of the fact that all the improvements in stage management since Shakespeare's time, whether in costume, lighting, enlargement of theatre decoration, music, or drop curtains, tend to delay the action and fix the attention of the audience on something besides the story.

ON THE STAGE

You cannot keep Shakespeare off the stage. The plays veer toward the boards as ducks veer toward the water when passing a pond; and this lurch is felt, not only in the whole drift and action of a play, but in its scenes and incidents, its decorative passages, its dumb show. These dramas excite the dramatic ambitions of every reader, they create good actors, and they have maddened the bad ones in all ages. Little scenes cut out of them are thrilling if properly done; and the great speeches, soliloquies, and harangues are the best monologues in existence. No actor has ever given a final interpretation of any one of the great rôles. Even when they are murdered by bad actors, they come to life again, as true creatures of the stage should do. The rôles are so elastic and so theatrical that they encourage bad acting. Let a man point up the speeches and pause for applause, and he gets it.

There is much in all the Elizabethan dramas, including Shakespeare's own, which encourages rant. Exaggeration, whether of laughter or of tears, is a dramatic element. To tear a passion to tatters is a human need, and clowns have always "laughed themselves, in order to set on some quantity of barren spectators to laugh, too." It is partly because Shakespeare lends himself to dramatic abuses, and is himself a "sweet, sweet poison to the age's tooth," that he has survived. Indeed Hamlet's advice to the players is at war with Shakespeare's own style, and with the spirit of English literature. It is Shakespeare himself, who, in a warning against excess, gives us one of the best examples of excess in all literature: —

Therefore, to be possess'd with double pomp,
To guard a title that was rich before,
To gild refined gold, to paint the lily,
To throw a perfume on the violet,
To smooth the ice, or add another hue
Unto the rainbow, or with taper-light
To seek the beauteous eye of heaven to garnish,
Is wasteful and ridiculous excess.

Hamlet's advice to the players is a pretty speech by an amateur, "For in the torrent and tempest and, as I may say, whirlwind of your passion, you must acquire and beget a temperance that shall give it smoothness!" But the tragedies of "Macbeth," "King Lear," and "Richard III" were not written by a man who was "acquiring and begetting temperance of expression"; and I should hate to see them played by an actor who took Hamlet's advice seriously. The tragedians of all nations have found that Shakespeare's storms will stand bellowing, and that overacting does not kill the plays, which respond like blooded chargers under the spur — nay, they run away with their riders, while the audience enjoys the sport.

The question of how to act Shakespeare is an open question; for no one has as yet appeared who was powerful enough to shut it. Iago is excellent as a sharp-eyed American gambler, or as a bluff Italian innkeeper. Richard III will hold an audience as a gladiator with a talent for rant, or as a sickly, embittered hunchback of the malevolent introspective type. He could hold the stage if he should play the tyrant in one scene and the sycophant in the next. There is an incomprehensible power behind the text in Shakespeare's rôles, which no acting can wholly obscure. Here 's a man that studies Benedick till he conjures a modern clubman out of an old cavalier. Here 's a Katherine who is at heart a soft, gentle creature, and dead in love with Petruchio all the while.

I once saw Hamlet played in German, by a Pole, a Jewish youth five feet high, desperately excitable, and more determinedly out of his mind than is possible outside of Poland. And yet unexpected sparks shone in the performance, and new demons danced. Certainly these plays overstimulate humanity; and inasmuch as they have driven many learned men mad in all ages, we ought not to be surprised if they excite the actors. The "judicious" may "grieve," as they sit in the best seats watching some termagant splitting the ears of the groundlings; but the judicious get an amusement of their own from the performance; for grieving is the chief joy of the judicious.

Ever since Charles Lamb's time there have been people who were so enraptured by reading Shakespeare to themselves and so pained when they saw him on the stage, that they thought the plays ought not to be acted at all. "I mean no disrespect to any actor," says Lamb, "but the sort of pleasure which Shakespeare's plays give in the acting seems to me not at all to differ from that which the audience receives from those of other writers; and they being in themselves essentially so different from others, I must conclude that there is something in the nature of acting that levels all distinctions."

Lamb develops the paradox with his usual sprightliness. This class of Shakespeare-lovers regard literary beauty as the main end of drama. They have known the text by heart since childhood; the romances already inhabit their imagination. When at a play they either shut their eyes, or open them upon what looks to them like a new and ugly world.

It is true that there are meanings in Shakespeare that cannot be gleaned in the theatre; for the drop scenes, furniture, lights, and music interrupt his ceaseless, intimate, bubbling, flashing exuberance. Nevertheless, the man in the playhouse, who receives his impressions through his eyes and ears, is the best judge of the story as drama, because he sees it as drama. There are, in fact, two techniques in Shakespeare, — the literary and the dramatic, — and the expert in one of these arts is apt to be inexpert in the other. Each of these interwoven arts is done with such mastery that the devotees of one hardly suspect the existence of the other. The dramatic interest is carried by the operation of sunken batteries and dynamos of dramatic appeal, whose power is lost upon those who, when they see a play, are really trying to re-read the play in a theatre.

Whether he was quite aware of it or not, Shakespeare wrote for a reading public as well as for the stage; and, indeed, in his day the passion for reading plays was as strong as the passion for seeing them acted. It must be confessed that some of his work is so subtle that it can be seen only in a half-light and does not carry on the modern stage. For instance, in "Antony and Cleopatra" a messenger enters. Cleopatra greets him with, —

How much unlike thou art to Antony,
Yet, coming from him, that great medicine hath
With his tinct gilded thee.

For the fraction of a second Cleopatra almost *sees* Antony, and Shakespeare records the impression. This sort of intimate thought-reading runs throughout the plays. The speeches are ripples on the surface. The characters are in mesmeric communication with one another; the creator has seen the drama, byplay and all, and much occurs in penumbra, which we grasp by instinct in the reading, but which fails to cross the footlights in the theatre. If a spectator, at the moment of Cleopatra's exclamation, happens to be wondering where the devil the stage decorator found his model for the glaring lotus capital, and whether Cleopatra really lived in the temple of Karnak, the point of her speech will be lost.

One of Shakespeare's greatest talents is his power of giving what passes in the minds of uneducated persons, of very old people, of drunken people. He catches the incalculable half-thoughts that glimmer in confused and ignorant minds. In his clowns and gravediggers, his Audreys, Dogberrys, and Pistols, he generally touches up the language into stage exaggeration: the misuse of words is dramatized. But there are places in which he leaves nature naked, as when the Hostess describes the death of Sir John Falstaff in "Henry IV, Part 2." This page is one of the greatest that Shakespeare ever penned; but the scene is not effective on the stage. Nor is Justice Shallow, in the same play, effective on the stage, when he gives that exhibition of the faint garrulousness of extreme old age. He must be thought of as standing on the green before his country house in remote Gloucestershire. In his babble there sounds a note of the lyre that no hand but Shakespeare's, whether Christian or pagan, ever struck. Such scenes are unstageable, and, if you point them up in the production, they lose their charm.

Sometimes a reader like Lamb will get an incommunicable joy from a single word ejaculated by one of Shakespeare's clowns; as where Andrew Aguecheek cries out against Malvolio, "Fie upon him, Jezebel!" Now, Sir Andrew has at some time in his early education heard the Bible story about Jezebel, and remembers the name vaguely as that of an impious, intolerable character. In the excitement of his shrill and feeble mind, Jezebel comes to him as the strongest word he can think of. There are, moreover, scenes in Shakespeare, and sometimes long scenes, which are brilliant as literature but not as drama; as, for instance, the Tavern scene, during which Pistol is thrown downstairs, in "Henry IV, Part 2." This belongs to the world of Fielding, Smollett, and Dickens, and as fiction it is greater than any of them; but it does not show in its best colors when staged. Let any reader turn to the "Two Gentlemen of Verona" and read the speech of Launce to his dog, in Act IV, Scene 4. Shakespeare wishes to amuse the audience between two poetic scenes, and gives us a little gem, a masterpiece; but it is literature, not drama.

For a generation all the fine arts have been languishing, and among them the poetic drama. We used to take Shakespeare for granted, because there had always been players in the offing, actors and companies, who drifted in and could recite "Lear" or "Macbeth" as readily as the player recites the speech about rugged Pyrrhus before the young Hamlet. So living was the tradition of Shakespeare, that we never stopped to think that the mere delivery of his lines was an art whose origin was to be traced to the age when the plays were written, and to a time when all the fine arts were taught in workshops and learned by apprentices under a master's eye. So unbroken has been the succession of great actors and of their companies, that we never pause to remember that we possess in them a living example of the mediæval system, that system which certain modern enthusiasts have sought in vain to revive in connection with painting and the handicrafts. The actor has always begun work as a member of a household academy which he entered as a youth, like the apprentices of old. When, in mature life, the actor detached himself from his troupe to found a company of his own, he merely floated off from the organism of a living tradition, and continued to perfect it under forms which had become second nature to him.

The craft and guild of acting have been preserved, as it were, by Shakespeare's stage family. The tones of the first actor who ever played the Ghost in "Hamlet" still sound upon our stage, and the actor is supposed to have been Shakespeare himself. Every actor of prominence, since the times of Elizabeth, has received his schooling in the whole cycle of the Shakespearean plays through this domestic system, and by being steeped in their atmosphere in early life.

It may be doubted whether, in teaching the fine

arts, academic influences of any kind can replace this old system of apprenticeship. The decay of painting began in the middle of the eighteenth century, when exhibitions, expert criticism, and theories of art came into fashion. Art was becoming exotic, a thing over which taste presided and theories hovered. People have been wondering what art is, ever since they left off regarding it as a trade and a "mystery," a thing made up of knacks, habits, and secrets, communicated, one hardly knew how, by the master to the apprentice, who watched and imitated the master's procedure, helped him on the work in hand, and imbibed rather than learned the technical part of his profession — a part not separated in the mind of anyone from its spiritual meaning. To be sure, a faint survival of the old system may be seen in the modern practice of painters, who allow their admirers to work in studios which the master visits, making comments on the work done by the aspirants, somewhat as a swimming-master might stand on the bank and make comments on the progress of young porpoises. But the old family life is gone, the bonds of art are broken between each two generations, and theory takes the place of tradition.

If the tradition of Shakespeare be once lost it will have to be sought for by a labor like that of digging in Pompeii to find frescoes: the meaning and the naturalness of the craft will never be quite recovered. I wonder what a revival of the "Tempest" or "Macbeth" would be like, if given by men who had got all their Shakespeare from books. The plays are full of stage secrets which books cannot preserve, and which are beginning to perish to-day like sea urchins at low tide. They have been expounded and illuminated during eight generations by the genius of great actors, whose interpretations have become almost a part of their text. The very glances and byplay of Betterton and Garrick and Kemble and Booth ought to shine all through a performance of "Hamlet"; and if these things be forgotten by posterity, a chapter of the human spirit will be lost. To the legatees of the old school we must still go for our staging of Shakespeare. We must graft upon living stock. It will not do to wait until the old fires are extinct, and then found an academy to revive them. A Shakespeare revival is already overdue, and the sooner it comes the more brilliantly will it blossom. It should come before the heart of the older tradition is cold. The practices of earlier masters may seem to the great public to be worn-out and unnecessary things, but to the artists they represent inspiration.

The staging of Shakespeare is not a case for dogmatism or for historic correctness, or a case for verbal piety. The plays cannot be produced textually, and they differ so widely from one another that there is a special atmosphere in each of them. We must suffer ourselves to be caught by the spirit — and then tread lightly. The bareness of the surroundings in which they were born is the very thing that forced all their genius to express itself in language. And we ought, I suppose, to rely upon *language* for our effects, so far as modern fashions will permit. But even here our convictions must amount to a mere tendency, not to a method.

Shakespeare had many different styles; he worked rapidly, experimented, indulged his humors, and ran through the gamut of possible ways of writing. He will pass from prose to poetry in the middle of a scene, in the middle of a sentence, and the general quality of his work is improvisation. The commentators dislike to hear this said, because they are men of leisure, of paste-pots and scissors, and cannot conceive of rapid thought. But it is likely that Shakespeare, during an afternoon walk, and before he began writing a play, was visited by the angels, the wraiths and prophetic intimations of the characters and situations which, later, in the good plays at least, welled up under his pen in all their complexity and perfection. No mind can "put together" such a play as "King Lear." The proof is that you cannot take it apart. You do not know where the joints are. Shakespeare thus keeps us all as fluid as he was himself; and whether we read him or act him, he keeps telling us: "You can live in me, but you cannot catch me."

IV

ROMEO AND JULIET

THOSE who know tell us that there is more money in "Romeo and Juliet" than in any other play on the boards. This does credit to human nature, for "Romeo and Juliet" is a most simple-hearted, romantic love-story, all one single plan of action, incident, and catastrophe. The tale itself triumphs. People follow it to-day much as its first auditors followed it — more nearly so perhaps than they can follow any other tale of Shakespeare. It is swifter, hotter, younger than the "Tempest" or "Cymbeline." In vain did Mrs. Kemble exclaim that no woman who was young enough to act Juliet could ever have acquired art enough to act her well. The young ones please: Juliet's lines set their aureole on the brow of youth. The sight of their young cheeks and the sound of their young voices carry the illusion, and we accept any immaturities in the acting as a part of the character. It is the same with Ophelia, if indeed one can call Ophelia a rôle; for Ophelia never gets on the stage at all, but remains in the mind as a ballad, a legend, an experience.

"Romeo and Juliet" is Shakespeare's triumph over the actors, for he has written a story of such convincing interest that the actors cannot spoil the narrative. He has given them hardly a chance to show their good points, or work up "conceptions" of the rôles. Yet he has given them just a hook or two on which to hang stage characters, and they almost always hang bogies on these hooks, to the damage of the play. Their main chance lies in Mercutio. I have in my life seen only one Mercutio who played the part so rapidly and naturally as to keep it in the background and make it a mere foil to Romeo. For Mercutio is not a character, but a supplement — the missing part of Romeo. It takes both of them to make a gay gallant. Mercutio is the phantasm that leaps from the brain of Shakespeare when his mind has been fatigued and a little disgusted with the monotonous egotism of his lovesick, over-romantic hero. This witty, cynical, galvanic Mercutio lashes himself into obscenity at the mere sight of Romeo. What a relief he is! But he must flash and vanish; he is only a recreation, a shaft of sunlight on a passing cloud. Let him not try to stay the heavens and drag out his business. At the back of the stage in all these plays, there is a demon in Shakespeare's employ working a machine that emits soft mysterious lightnings. We must not kill his work with our crude antics and modern apparatus. No one who is reading a play to himself will allow the entire show to be held up while Mercutio stages Queen Mab, or Jaques produces a conscientious pantomime of the Seven Ages of Man, which turns under his treatment into a lesson in burlesque.

The *vignettes* in Shakespeare must be lightly handled. Hamlet's speech to the players, Iago's picture of the good woman, Katherine's portrait of Wolsey, and his other roulades of wit, must be flung off, — or tossed or smiled or handed or dropped off, — but never ground in. It requires the most consummate art to do these things in a way that is both thrilling and casual. Mercutio is the first of the actor's pitfalls in "Romeo and Juliet"; and the second is the Nurse. One always gets a little too much of this person. She is invaluable, of course, but her value should be economized. The manager would do well to have a talk with her beforehand, saying, "Madam, we cannot stage this play without a nurse; but if your idea is to occupy the centre of the stage and play at dolls with your part, I shall do with you just as I did with Polonius yesterday—get another."

The best points in Shakespeare are sometimes not made by the actors at all, but fall *between* the cues, and are thrilling because of the situation which they create. The Nurse's lines contain one such climax, and it is one of the great strokes of dramatic genius in the play. It is a climax tragic in its import, natural in its manner, unforeseen and startling in its power. This is where the Nurse advises Juliet to marry Paris, although she knows that Juliet has been married to Romeo some three hours before:—

NURSE

Faith here it is,
Romeo is banish'd and all the world to nothing
That he dares ne'er come back to challenge ye
Or if he do, it needs must be by stealth.
Then since the case so stand as now it doth,
I think it best you married with the county;
Romeo 's a dishclout to him,—etc.

Juliet conceals her horror at the proposition till the Nurse has left the room, and then breaks out with

Ancient damnation! O most wicked fiend,—etc.

The commonplace naturalism of the base-hearted old cockney woman is a thing unlooked for in tragedy. It is a bit of realism thrust in among dithyrambs. If you should work over the point and try to make much of it, you would spoil it. It must pass with the rest. Shakespeare has here allowed his whole plot to hinge on what seems to be the whim of an underling. It is the Nurse's conduct that determines Juliet to pursue her tragic course, and makes her step into the mill-race. And yet scarcely anything is said about the matter at the moment it occurs on the stage. No other dramatist has transitions of this kind, — turns of thought that are unexpected, fleeting, profound, — so delicate that they must be instrumented with an æolian harp; and yet there is thunder in them. The plot pivots on them.

One of these shifts, from one kind of dramatic appeal to another, and where the lightning from on high falls between the characters on the stage, occurs in Hamlet's interview with his mother, where, in the midst of the towering passion of both Hamlet and his mother, Hamlet sees the Ghost. The Queen for a moment really believes Hamlet to be mad: she forgets her moral agonies and becomes plainly a frightened woman. All she has to say is, "Alas, he's mad!" This naturalism, which comes crashing down from the tragic roof in Shakespeare, is what makes his writing different from any other writing on earth. If you surround his dramas with pomp, as if they were the work of Æschylus or Corneille, you will lose him. The barn floor must be under the feet of the actor. Nothing else is humble enough, home-bred, earthy, and inward enough, to show the fall of his fires.

V

RICHARD III

This play is a rattling melodrama — perhaps the first good melodrama written in England, for its immediate popularity was immense and five editions appeared during Shakespeare's lifetime. It is boisterous and stagy, — almost an extravaganza, — and would be intolerable but for the wonderful godlike humor that pervades it. There is, to my mind, no note of tragedy in it; for the tragic themes have been handled wholesale, and as if by a giant at play. The characters seem to clamor for the boards. If you delay them, and insist on understanding the Dramatis Personæ, seeking to identify each of them historically, you will waste your time. The British Royal Family in Richard's time was so multitudinous and complicated that even Shakespeare himself makes mistakes in it; and this though he had spent several years over the chronicles while writing his historical plays. But as soon as the feet of the actors touch the boards, the characters in "Richard III" identify themselves very readily. Their names are announced as they enter. "But who comes here? The new-delivered Hastings." "Here come the lords of Buckingham and Derby," etc.

In the opening scenes it is dinned into the audience that Henry VI and his son have been murdered by Richard before the play opens; and the other people to be murdered pass toward their execution so rapidly after their first appearance, that we never confuse them. Most of the victims are allowed time to stop and point out that the curse has come upon them, which curse has been provided very unmistakably in a long scene near the beginning of the play. This curse helps hold the play together, and it is, as any child can see, the curse of the old Queen Margaret, whom the rest of the company have supplanted. But if by chance you fall into any doubt about the identity of the murdered people, your mind will be set at rest by a recapitulation. On the night before the battle the eleven ghosts rise in the order of their taking-off, and each pronounces a malediction on Richard, who is asleep on one side of the stage, and a blessing on Richmond (who, by the way, was Queen Elizabeth's grandfather), who is asleep on the other side of the stage. So well did Shakespeare understand the art of clear dramatic presentation.

Most of the scenes in this play are conceived in the same spirit of outrageous dramatic clarity that is seen in Richard's opening of "Now is the winter of our discontent," etc. Richard is "determinèd to prove a villain." Many separate scenes are little dramatic unities in themselves, full of points, full of stage business. The style of the play is so easily imitated that Colley Cibber doctored it to the extent of two thousand lines, and his version held the stage for one hundred and twenty years. Two of Cibber's improvements,—"Off with his head, So much for Buckingham!" and "Richard 's himself again!" have passed into the language as a part of Shakespeare. The style of the play is, indeed, that of the babes in the wood; and some learned critics have supposed that the ballad lies at the foundation of the play. I think so myself. That is why "Richard III" is popular, that is how it is good. That is why schoolboys spout it, and great actors chafe and fume till they can show themselves off in it. The play gives everyone a chance. Clarence's dream is surely enough to satisfy any reasonable actor for a season. Buckingham and Hastings have telling rôles and dying speeches. There are four women's parts, every one of them towering with stage possibilities.

Let us not forget those very endearing murderers of Clarence. These gentle cockneys belong to the grave-digging peasantry, the argumentative yokels, and alehouse loafers of Shakespeare's comedy. In "Hamlet" such figures are used as mere decoration, but in "Richard III" they must be melodramatic, like everything in the play. The murder is well managed. There is a soft villian and a hard villain; we are kept in doubt as to the outcome, and the blow is struck unexpectedly with a "Look behind you!" in the true, time-honored manner.

In writing "Richard III" Shakespeare did not deny himself any stage effects that he could think of. The murder of Clarence, the funeral procession of a king, a throne-room scene, the cursing of Richard by his mother, two bad dreams, two orations (one to each army by its commander), a desperate battle scene with Richard shouting for his horse, and the final entry of Richmond bearing the crown, and making the very gratifying announcement, "The bloody dog is dead!" Of course there are messengers. When the murders begin to run short, at the close of the fourth act, five messengers come in one after the other to announce the coming battle. This shows Shakespeare's mood,—his conception of the play,—and we may take these messengers as a hint of the spirit in which the play as a whole should be given.

Anæmic persons may mutter that two murders are not so terrible as one, and eleven ghosts not so terrifying as one, and that many curses are not so impressive as one — for it appears that the terrible Queen Margaret is herself under a curse; and this, with her own curses and the curse of Richard by his mother, makes a perfect cloud of curses that are in the air. But Shakespeare did not regard such things as overstepping the modesty of nature. He enjoyed quantity,—in ghosts as in other things,—when the mood was on him; and this play, with its universal popularity, is the best answer ever given to a kind of parlor art-criticism, which is as old as Aristotle and of which Hamlet's advice to the players is a sample. It is clear that "Richard III" is a sort of greenroomful of properties. The actors and managers do well to use such of them as they can, cutting them to fit the occasion; for some of them are impossible on the modern stage, and must always have been feeble, as, for instance, the scenes of antiphonal wailing, where the characters repeat the same phrases after each other in an operatic manner.

The character of Richard has caused the literary people many wakeful nights. No one has ever seen a man like Richard III; and yet he is nearly perfect as a stage villain. He is glowing with wit and humor, and in his seven soliloquies he expounds himself like a prologue. One thing however is clear: Had

Richard been gloomy, the play would have become a bore. We should have cried, "Oh, here he comes again, that dreary criminal!" I doubt whether Shakespeare troubled himself much about the question, Do such persons exist? or built up his characters out of observation. He evolved them rather through stage experience.

Jeremiah Mason, the great jury lawyer, was asked by a friend at the close of a murder trial, in which he had given proofs of phenomenal power in defending a criminal, "What are your personal beliefs as to the man's guilt?" "Why," said Mason, "I have never given a thought to the matter." We ought to remember this story in criticizing any character in a drama. The stage, like the law, has its fictions, its presumptions; it has an appeal and a forensic of its own; and though human nature as it exists has, no doubt, been translated into this language by the playwright and for stage purposes, you can never go to the stage language and translate it back again into life.

Richard III's courtship of Anne goes well on the stage; it has interested the onlookers for several hundred years, and there must therefore be some kind of symbolic truth in the scene; but to compare it to a scene in real life, or to compare any character in Shakespeare to any real character, is absurd. One might as reasonably take a stage helmet or stage cup of poison and try to relate it to real life. All our painstaking discussions of Shakespeare's people as human characters must go by the board. The plays should be acted largely, as they were written. I think that even Salvini and Irving would have done better if they had been less conscientious and intentional. Richard should be played genially and with gusto, and without so much regard to a supposed inner logic of character as to the blatant outer logic of stage effects. For instance: the terror and repentance of Richard during his bad night before the battle were laid on with a trowel by Shakespeare for the sake of the gallery. The speech is crude in detail, for Richard suddenly discovers that *nobody loves him*, and says, "Is there a murderer here? No. Yes. I am. Then fly!" etc. But the speech is right in the large. The bad man of a play ought to call for drink before a battle, and be tortured by remorse in his dreams; the good man ought to say his prayers and be visited by angels. If it were n't for such touches as this, and the stage experience behind them, "Richard III" would never have held the boards since 1593.

VI

HAMLET

THE so-called laws of dramatic writing, which have been discussed and expounded ever since the time of Aristotle, were not discovered by men who spent their evenings at a variety show. These laws were first given out by scholars, who found themselves very comfortable with someone else's manuscript spread before them and a good light flowing over their shoulder, but who would have been extremely uncomfortable if they had been obliged to put together a play that should entertain a mixed audience for a couple of hours. I scarcely know what it is that puts the critic above the author, and provides him with his historic and invulnerable complacency; but I think it is due to leisure and the cheapness of writing materials.

The admirable notice on Shakespeare in the Encyclopædia Britannica is marred by a few condescending sentences of æsthetic criticism, of which I give the most imposing. After pointing out some of Shakespeare's deficiencies, the critic continues: —

This want of finish, this imperfect fusing of the literary ore, is essentially characteristic of the Renaissance, as compared with ages in which the creative impulse is weaker, and leaves room for a finer concentration of the means upon the end. There is nearly always unity of purpose in a Shakespearean play, but it often requires an intellectual effort to grasp it, and does not result in a unity of effect. The issues are obscured by a careless generosity, which would extend to art the boundless freedom of life itself. Hence the intrusive and jarring elements which stand in such curious incongruity with the utmost reaches of which the dramatic spirit is capable; the conventional and melodramatic endings, the inconsistencies of action and even of character, the emotional confusions of tragi-comedy, the complications of plot and subplot, the marring of the give-and-take of dialogue by superfluities of description and of argument, the jest and bombast lightly thrown in to suit the taste of the groundlings, all the flecks that to an instructed modern criticism are only tôo apparent upon the Shakespearean sun. It perhaps follows from this that the most fruitful way of approaching Shakespeare is by an analysis of his work rather as a process than as a completed whole.

"An instructed modern criticism"! But the devil of it is to discover just what these "too apparent flecks" are, and then to whisk them deftly into the waste-paper basket, leaving the "literary finish," which the critic understands so well. Molière, who was one of the most sensible of men, and who lived in an age of pseudo-classicism which frostbit all the genius of France except his own, took the instructed modern criticism of his times quite cheerfully. He says: —

Je me fierois assez à l'approbation du parterre, par la raison qu'entre ceux qui le composent il y en a plusieurs qui sont capable de juger d'une pièce selon les règles, et que les autres en jugent par la bonne façon d'en juger, qui est de se laisser prendre aux choses, et de n'avoir ni prévention aveugle, ni complaisance affectée, ni delicatesse ridicule.

There is in reality only one dramatic law. We can see that it must exist, yet no one has ever been able to formulate it. The gist of it is as follows: Something must happen on the stage that interests the audience; otherwise, they will go away.

As for the old, sacred apparatus of criticism, of which Shakespeare knew nothing, we need make no long delay over its theories. One or two of his tragedies can, with a little stretching of the tent-pins, be dragged in under the roof of classic and pseudo-classic criticism. For instance, we can say of "King Lear" that the theme is Greek; for, as everyone knows, the regular theme of Greek tragedy was the punishment of self-will, of insolence and impiety. Now the play of "King Lear" deals with this same idea — self-will — seen from the opposite side. The play represents the triumph of humility, and Lear is a reformed tyrant. We can say of "King Lear" that it is a single, grand symphonic poem: the attention of everyone is held to one single idea during the entire evening. The author takes the audience into his confidence; the climaxes are foreseen and led up to.

In observing these matters, we lull ourselves into a belief that something is known about the laws of the drama. If, however, we turn to "Hamlet," we find that Shakespeare has produced effects as remarkable as those of "King Lear" by the use of a technique that seems to be entirely different. Shakespeare indeed improvises his technique. It is never twice alike, and he is as great when he appears to be violating all the supposed rules of dramatic writing as he is when he seems to be following at least some of them.

"Hamlet" is the most famous play in the world.

It excites the learned as much as it delights the vulgar. It is the most stageable invention ever put together by the wit of man; and yet nobody quite knows what the theme of it is, or what the moral is — if it has a moral. The execution of the work is so brilliant that it dazzles us, and we cannot see just how much is structure and how much ornament. The world has been searching for two hundred years for a bit of smoked glass through which to look at "Hamlet." Its popularity on the stage is easy to understand: it is the richest variety show in existence. You have a murder and a ghost to begin with, and in the course of the play you have seven more murders and a suicide. You have Ophelia, Polonius, a play within a play, an insurrection, the gravediggers, a funeral, a hand-to-hand fight in a grave, a pretended fencing-bout which is really a duel, and, finally, the grand collapse of the whole kingdom, the extinction of its royal family, and the martial entrance of a conqueror who views a stage on which dead bodies are piled.

Certainly if such a feast of excitement does not satisfy the theatre-goer, nothing will; for these scenes drift by him as in a dream, and are each so interesting and startling, so witty and amusing in themselves, so full of tears and heart-break, that the onlooker never discovers that the play has no action in the dramatic sense of the word. Nothing has happened in the Story-of-Hamlet's-Revenge between the first act, where the theme is so gorgeously announced, and the very end when the King is killed.

What is it, then, that holds all these thrilling scenes together, and makes people watch and gape and wonder what is coming next, and go night after night to see a story which is merely the dramatization of a mental paralysis, a series of actions that depict inaction? If Shakespeare had shown his scenario and explained his plan to any competent and instructed playwright, the scholar would have said: —

"But my dear fellow, this will never do. You begin the play as if it were a ghost-fate-drama, and then your ghost and his story are completely forgotten. The actor who plays the ghost goes home at the end of the third act. That ghost ought to appear in the climax at the end. But it seems that you have just used the ghost to help get your play under way. That's not a proper way to treat a ghost. Then you kill off your heroine in the middle: your heroine, like your ghost, is a mere makeweight. Then, you must know, that the first rule is that a playwright should never equivocate: he must explain each step. But with you everything is equivocation. Is Hamlet really mad? Does Ophelia drown herself out of grief for her father or out of love for Hamlet? Did the Queen know that her first husband was murdered? Moreover, you should never surprise an audience. In this play you jounce your audience from one surprise to another. The first is when Hamlet changes his mind after seeing the ghost, and suddenly determines not to tell Horatio about it; this amazes the pit. The audience is surprised again when he changes his mind the next morning and confides in Horatio. It is surprised by the murder of Polonius, by the banishment of Hamlet, by his return, by every incident in the play. Nothing is prepared for. Then again, why kill off that amusing Polonius? Then again, you make your hero commit three cold-blooded murders. Why did you do that? It destroys all sympathy for him. The play is an amateur play, my boy."

What is the single thought that lies behind the drama of "Hamlet"? Let us listen to the gossip of the audience at the close of the play, and while the people are walking home to supper. "Hamlet" excites the same emotion in all minds. Goethe and Coleridge and Victor Hugo are talking about the same question that agitates the peanut gallery: Why could n't the young man avenge his father's murder? Surely the brain and consciousness of these listeners must have been undergoing stroke after stroke from some divine apparatus, the blows must have been falling in the same place on some harmonic anvil, or this tremendous unitary effect on the audience could not have been produced.

Is the *continuity of inaction* such an idea as can hold an audience spellbound, when exhibited in various vivid scenes of melodrama, each of which calls for some action that does not come? "To be or not to be," which the world has seized on as the key to the play, would lead one to think so. The unity in "Hamlet" consists in the succession of episodes in which Hamlet always disappoints expectation. The man cannot act, but only feel, reflect, and plan. He is, however, constantly exciting us into a belief that he is about to do something; but the action he takes is never a deed; it is a mere gesture. His actions consist in (1) the ruse to catch the conscience of a king; (2) the murder of Polonius at a moment when he cannot *see* Polonius; (3) the forging of a document that is to cost his schoolmates their lives; and (4) the murder of the King, to which he seems spurred at the last moment by personal vengeance and at a moment when he knows he is dying of the King's poison. These deeds are not deeds, but spasms.

The miracle in the play is the fact that we see the same spectre behind and through each climax of the melodrama. We do not know quite what that figure is, yet it is terrific. The same spectre is flashed into our minds through a succession of different poetic mists: we feel its identity, yet we cannot name the wraith. The variety in the drama is due to the different kinds of poetic atmosphere with which Shakespeare has clothed his spectre under different circumstances. Perhaps it is the isolation of Hamlet's mind that is being exhibited in each case — an isolation somehow connected with his incapacity for action.

Let us consider the different kinds of poetic mystery in which Hamlet's spirit is enveloped in the several scenes of the play. You have, in the first place, the two great tragic scenes: the opening scene with the Ghost, and Hamlet's interview with his mother at the end of the third act. Both of these scenes are drenched in precisely the same kind of poetry. They have an atmosphere of their own, which appears nowhere else in the play. You have, next, Hamlet's wit and banter, the badinage with which he meets all the minor personages of the piece. This is sometimes sharp, often good-natured, always inward and remote. It resembles the talk of a man who is talking to himself. His words are non-responsive to his interlocutor, but interesting to us because we know what the subject of his thought really is. This banter emphasizes the chasm of contemplation in which Hamlet is sunk. He is alone, and his solitude is dramatized by every word he speaks. You have, next, those great soliloquies, in which the spiritual isolation of the man is articulated with such accuracy of analysis and such eloquence that they have become Biblical. They take rank with the Psalms in the popular life of the world as the cry of a solitary spirit. These soliloquies are so wonderful that we hardly notice that they are replicas of one another. Let anyone read the soliloquy (Act IV, Scene 4) on a plain in Denmark, and find an idea which has not been more hotly and convincingly expressed in "O what a rogue and peasant slave am I!" This scene on the plain has been planned as a setting for this soliloquy. It has no other function. It is not wholly successful, because the soliloquy is too purely a repetition.

You have, next, the scenes showing Hamlet's relations with Ophelia, which are certainly the most moving scenes in the play. They have an appeal in them, and a kind of poetry which is entirely their own. Hamlet is isolated even from Ophelia. Some people think that this is due to the shock he received by the Ghost's revelations. But the cause is deeper; that shock only revealed his native and almost accursed isolation. He seems to think he *might have* loved Ophelia. When, later, he jumps into the grave, he says he *had* loved her; but he never mentions her thereafter. Then again, in the interviews with Horatio, Hamlet shows a deep and somewhat feminine pathos about himself; a distinct, new poetic note is sounded in these scenes and nowhere else. In spite of Hamlet's tremendous emotionalism about his parents, and in spite of his love for Horatio, there is a certain lack of heart in him. He is pathetic and a little monstrous. We pity, but can hardly love the isolated man.

Whatever may be the reason, the play of "Hamlet" makes a different and more personal appeal than any other play. Everyone fancies himself a Hamlet. There is, indeed, some shadow of Hamlet in everyone; and this is the shadow that Shakespeare has been casting upon the cloudy air. He has seen it among the elemental forces in his own mind — it is the Contemplator.

Consider what happens daily to us all. Between contemplation and action there comes normally a change of mood; a lever is pulled, a new gear is brought into play. With Hamlet the lever is pulled and nothing happens: a lobe of his brain is missing. When he is knocked down by a fact, he is like a horse that cannot get up again. After his interview with the Ghost he knows only one thing. He will do nothing. He will not reveal anything; he must wait. And so on: every time that Hamlet shies at a resolution or baulks at a conclusion, the drama is intensified.

Had Hamlet been represented as a bad man or a cynic, no one would have been mystified by him. Everyone would have said, "His incapacity is the punishment of sin." But Hamlet is good. The play does not concern the hiatus between Good and Evil, but between Mind and Will. The problem is subtle, yet the elements are as universal as the devil himself. Hence the wide appeal made by the play.

The theme of "Hamlet" is grief — for all of Hamlet's feelings turn to grief: his love is grief; his friendship is grief; his humor is grief. It is a peculiar, withering sort of grief — perhaps unmanly grief; at any rate, the kind of grief that closes the petals of the heart and holds them shut till the soul is dead. In the last two scenes of the drama, Hamlet has lost his charm. He is washed out, spiritless, uninteresting. Does Shakespeare intend this? I hardly think so. I think that, in the long scene in which Hamlet gives Horatio an account of his English trip, Shakespeare is trying to entertain the audience; and that in the following very dreary scene, when Hamlet banters Osric, Shakespeare is trying to be amusing. In the final duel-and-death scene, Shakespeare makes a haggard attempt at a brilliant ending. But alas, the skyey influences will not have it so. They have already blown the theme into the sere and yellow. They have flapped the life out of his hero. Too well, too powerfully has the Muse whispered her inspiration to the poet and breathed into him the vision of a soul killed by inactivity and an enterprise sicklied o'er by a pale cast of thought. The tragedy is finished before the play ends. The tail-piece of the melodrama has no one's passion to support it, and there survives in Hamlet himself nothing but a few drops of weak pathos about his own fate.

VII

THE MERRY WIVES OF WINDSOR

"THE MERRY WIVES OF WINDSOR" has an interest of its own, because it belongs to an inferior variety of play and is unique among Shakespeare's dramas. It is a comedy of manners, not a romantic drama. The tradition that this play was written in two weeks, and at the request of Queen Elizabeth, for the sake of showing Falstaff in love, is quite probable, for both its plot and its characters are mechanical. Falstaff, Bardolph, The Hostess, etc. had been created by Shakespeare in "Henry IV, Part 1," and some of them had reappeared in "Henry IV, Part 2." They came into existence as make-weights, figures of low-comedy intended to balance the feudal romance of the main characters. As such, they had a life-glory of their own. They are spontaneous, inimitable, and they evidently became popular favorites immediately. In the "Merry Wives of Windsor" these same names are given to a set of *mannequins* who are put through their paces in a comedy, or farce, of intrigue.

The influence of court life thus hangs over the "Merry Wives," and that is why the story about Queen Elizabeth, whether true or false, has clung to the play. In reading it one cannot help realizing that the chief blessing of Shakespeare's destiny was that during his lifetime the stage was not taken seriously by the court. Lords and ladies have need of sophisticated amusements, conventional, well-understood entertainments, which are witty, smooth, and safe. The command of a sovereign is ever that a playwright repeat himself; and in this process of repetition a standard theatre comes into existence. And something, too, goes out of the playwright during the experience. The "Merry Wives of Windsor" bears to "Twelfth Night" the relation that a thing done to order bears to a thing that a man has done to please himself. The craftsman's part is admirable, but the poetry has gone out of the work. The "Merry Wives" is crammed with wit, and yet there is no charm in it, and the only bit of the old romantic drama it contains is the fairy scene at the end. Consider the Falstaff of the "Merry Wives," how shorn he is of that incredible spontaneity and surprise — the surprise to the man himself — that radiates through all of Falstaff's talk in "Henry IV." Consider Dame Quickly, the Hostess, who, in the "Merry Wives," is as clever and base-minded as ever; but she has become a type, and is no longer an individual, as she was in "Henry IV." Ford, the jealous husband, is a thing hacked out with a jack-knife; Shallow has lost his pathos; he repeats his old leads out of "Henry IV," where they were so beautiful, and brags of his youthful prowess, but without arousing our interest.

The whole play shows the influence of a disturbing force, and lurches toward the later comedy. It is as if Paul Veronese, being asked by a pope for an easel-piece, had done something in the style of Nicholas Poussin. It is as if Sophocles had written a play in the style of the later Greek Comedy of Manners.

THE MERRY WIVES OF WINDSOR

Shakespeare in this *tour-de-main* — the "Merry Wives" — reveals the organic nature of the link between romantic and sophisticated comedy. The result is due, perhaps, to sheer haste and indifference on Shakespeare's part. He retains the wit, slashes the characters into fixed types, and elaborates the plot. As a result you have the Comedy of Manners. In another age Shakespeare might easily have become a court dramatist. He would have turned out potboilers with as great facility as he turned out the "Tempest" and "Cymbeline."

VIII

OTHELLO AND HENRY V

"OTHELLO" is in one sense the most perfect work of art in literature. There is no excess in it — a thing most rare in Shakespeare. Every facet is true, and casts a ray upward and forward toward the distant focus and burning spot of the climax. For any speech in a play has a complex function. It must arise from the circumstance, explain a character and unfold it a little, oppose the context, move the story on a step, and be in itself something witty and agreeable, or something poetic and profound. Besides all this, it becomes second nature with a playwright to make his characters say things that have a double meaning — one for the audience and one for the stage characters.

And yet the perfection of Othello as a play has been gained at a certain sacrifice of romantic beauty. In "Othello" the inordinate powers of Shakespeare became concentrated upon stage technicalities as the main point. Everything is sacrificed to theatrical effect. There is thus more to be gained and less to be lost in seeing the play (as opposed to reading it), than with most of his dramas. Shakespeare has not been carried away with Desdemona as he is with Juliet and Ophelia and Imogen. Iago seems to be the author's favorite. Shakespeare is perfectly enchanted with Iago; and the character is, I confess, the best stage villain ever invented. Yet Iago is not a human being at all; he is not even a true stage character; he is a demon. By the sacrifice of one personage to diabolism and virtuosity, the greatest analyst of human character that the world has known found a framework about which the stage characters of his drama should dance. He obtained from Iago that sort of advantage that the Greek dramatists drew from their chorus, which kept punctuating the story with explanations. Iago has eight soliloquies, in which he explains the innumerable and very complex details on which Othello's suspicions are to hang. These soliloquies are the iron armature that holds up the group of sculpture. They are the centre of the action. They are the *sine qua non* of the drama. The story does not tell itself, as in "Romeo and Juliet," but is assisted by machinery.

Is there in the whole history of cynicism anything comparable to the eloquence and magical perfection of Iago's talk? Real cynicism is sad; Mephistopheles is a dried-up, middle-aged clubman; Milton's Satan is a rhetorician. But Iago is a black angel, full of leaping, spontaneous, electrical vitality. He is, in truth, the Spirit of Evil, with no passions and no habitation; and he ought to have been shown with horns and a tail. But the world has never noted this circumstance. The world accepts Iago as a man, and shudders, feeling nevertheless a little mystified and prejudiced against the play. It is a tragedy of intrigue, and Iago is a figure borrowed from comedy, a precursor of the Barber of Seville. We must not think that Shakespeare adopted his devil-machine intentionally: he was driven into it as a means of working the plot. In order to fulfill his function,

Iago must be ubiquitous, in touch with all classes, a social being, a privileged character. This is the reason why he has been compared to an innkeeper. Iago, being the showman of the piece, is never on an even footing with the other characters. The rest seem to be in a hypnotic conspiracy to proclaim him a fine fellow and friend to all. They talk like parrots, using the same words whenever they mention him. "Honest Iago"; "Iago is most honest"; "I never knew a Florentine more kind and honest"; "O that 's an honest fellow"; "Full of love and honesty"; "This honest creature"; "This fellow 's of exceeding honesty"; "Nay, stay, thou shouldst be honest"; "O brave Iago, honest and just"; "An honest man he is"; "My friend, thy husband, honest, honest Iago." All this is magnificent play-writing of the sign-board kind.

The scheme of "Othello" is somewhat obvious, somewhat mechanical, and the result is that the catastrophe seems to follow, not from fate or moral causes, but from the machinations of a purposeless devil. And this sharpness of touch is spread over the rest of the play. The dramatic points are everywhere rubbed in to the limit of human endurance. Desdemona is not merely too innocent, but in one place is flatly unnatural. This is where Othello is roaring for the handkerchief (Act III, Scene 4), and she refuses to explain. So also, Emilia, who has witnessed Othello's rage over the lost handkerchief, never explains the situation, although she is represented as a kind-hearted woman and had herself stolen the handkerchief. Particularly crude is the repetition of Iago's mode of dealing with his various dupes,

Roderigo, Othello, and Cassio. "I have professed myself thy friend and I confess me knit to thy deserving with cables of perdurable toughness; thou art sure of me"; "I protest in the sincerity of love and honest kindness"; "My lord, you know I love you," and so on.

Many other examples could be found to show the coarseness of Shakespeare's brush in "Othello." It is as if some painter with the technical equipment of Velasquez had done a masterpiece in which all the values were slightly forced. Almost every one of Edwin Booth's very remarkable notes on the play, which are printed in Dr. Furness's edition, consists of hints to the actors, telling them how to soften the text by forbearing to do the obvious thing: how to avoid being stagy.

The quantity of stage business in "Othello" injures the poetic temperament of the play as we read it, and almost reduces the great speeches in it to what used to be called the "Beauties of Shakespeare." Not so on the stage. On the stage the characters flock by us, talking and thinking, often talking to themselves, sometimes pursuing two trains of thought at once. Rapid short scenes following one another with no curtains between — what a system was this to give life to a play! As an example of swiftness take the second scene of Act I. There are two distinct search-parties who are out after Othello.

IAGO. He 's married.
CASSIO. To who?

(*Reënter* OTHELLO.)

IAGO. Marry, to — Come, Captain, will you go?

OTHELLO. Have with you.
CASSIO. Here comes another troop to seek for you.

When the plot once gets started, the pace at which it moves is really the pace at which Othello's suspicions develop. The audience is thinking about the inner problems; and I suppose there is nowhere in literature any picture of a passion that is so rapid in its progress as Othello's jealousy. It is like a prairie fire; and the externals of the action keep pace with it. Any page of the play will illustrate this; but I will cite two passages, which occur toward the end, and show on what a small scale the play must be conceived in order to be staged naturally. The scene in which Othello strikes Desdemona occurs just after he has had a seizure, and has fallen unconscious through passion. Lodovico has arrived from Venice with a letter, on which Othello tries in vain to fix his attention, while he is really thinking of Cassio, and listening to the talk of the others.

LODOVICO. The duke and senators of Venice greet you.
(*Gives him a letter.*)
OTHELLO. I kiss the instrument of their pleasures.
(*Opens the letter and reads.*)
DESDEMONA. And what 's the news, good cousin Lodovico?
IAGO. I am very glad to see you, signior;
Welcome to Cyprus.
LOD. I thank you. How does Lieutenant Cassio?
IAGO. Lives, sir.
DES. Cousin, there 's fallen between him and my lord
An unkind breach; but you shall make all well.
OTH. Are you sure of that?
DES. My lord?

OTH. (*reads*) "This fail you not to do, as you will —"
LOD. He did not call; he 's busy in the paper.
Is there division 'twixt my lord and Cassio?
DES. A most unhappy one: I would do much
To atone them, for the love I bear to Cassio.
OTH. Fire and brimstone!
DES. My lord?
OTH. Are you wise?
DES. What, is he angry?
LOD. May be the letter mov'd him;
For, as I think, they do command him home
Deputing Cassio in his government.
DES. By my troth, I am glad on 't.
OTH. Indeed?
DES. My lord?
OTH. I am glad to see you mad.
DES. Why, sweet Othello?
OTH. Devil! (*Striking her*)
DES. I have not deserv'd this.
LOD. My lord, this would not be believ'd in Venice,
Though I should swear I saw 't: 't is very much:
Make her amends; she weeps.

The characters are here as complex, and almost as inarticulate, as they would be in real life; and the whole thing passes in a moment. You cannot put stilts on such a scene, or recite it in Alexandrines: it is domestic tragedy.

The last act of "Othello" opens with a typical hurly-burly, which takes place in the dark, with persons entering and leaving at such a rate that no audience can keep track as to just what is happening. Eight characters are involved; one is killed; one wounded. The whole scene has been devised very cleverly, almost too cleverly, and is generally cut down in the acting; but perhaps the best way is to play it, and play it fast. These hurly-burlies are a conventional feature in Shakespeare, like the "tragic loading" of the stage with dead bodies in the finale. They have the qualities of the charade, and are most difficult to retain in a large modern theatre.

In order that we may get away for a moment from the lyrical Shakespeare of "Romeo and Juliet" and the playwright's Shakespeare of "Othello," let us jump to a style very dissimilar to both. In this way we may view the subject from a new perspective. When I was a boy, there was an actor called Rignold, who hired a few curtains, pasteboard castle walls, and painted wooden cannon, and gave the play of "Henry V." He was handsome and well-made, with a fine walk and presence, and was a magnificent reciter of blank verse. I cannot to-day read the great speeches of that play without hearing his voice and seeing his gestures. There was little in that whole performance to carry an audience, except Rignold's wonderful declamation; but it was enough. "Henry V" is one of the few dramas that can bear this treatment. The story moves very slowly like a pageant, like a series of frescoes accompanied by the music of stately, ornate, eloquent speeches, choruses, and rhapsodies. But how many persons living are there who can recite the following chorus (Act III, Prologue) and keep it interesting?

CHORUS. Thus with imagin'd wing our swift scene flies
In motion of no less celerity
Than that of thought. Suppose that you have seen
The well-appointed king at Hampton pier

Embark his royalty; and his brave fleet
With silken streamers the young Phœbus fanning:
Play with your fancies, and in them behold
Upon the hempen tackle ship-boys climbing;
Hear the shrill whistle which doth order give
To sounds confus'd; behold the threaden sails,
Borne with the invisible and creeping wind,
Draw the huge bottoms through the furrow'd sea,
Breasting the lofty surge: O, do but think
You stand upon the rivage and behold
A city on the inconstant billows dancing;
For so appears this fleet majestical,
Holding due course to Harfleur. Follow, follow:
Grapple your minds to sternage of this navy,
And leave your England, as dead midnight still,
Guarded with grandsires, babies, and old women,
Either past or not arriv'd to pith and puissance;
For who is he, whose chin is but enrich'd
With one appearing hair, that will not follow
These cull'd and choice-drawn cavaliers to France?
Work, work your thoughts, and therein see a siege;
Behold the ordnance on their carriages,
With fatal mouths gaping on girded Harfleur.
Suppose the ambassador from the French comes back;
Tells Harry that the king doth offer him
Katherine his daughter, and with her, to dowry,
Some petty and unprofitable dukedoms.
The offer likes not: and the nimble gunner
With linstock now the devilish cannon touches,
(*alarum, and chambers go off*)
And down goes all before them. Still, be kind,
And eke out our performance with your mind.

As spoken on Shakespeare's stage, to a small audience, which relied entirely on its imagination and was following the tale, this chorus, no doubt, floated by easily on its natural beauties. But to speak it before the curtain in a modern opera house, consuming, of course, twice the time that the lines formerly required, is a problem that would tax the elocution of Salvini. Not only must the actor's utterance be slower, but his gait and gestures, his thought and feeling, his whole art and craft must deal in fewer ideas and in a larger symbolism than the earlier stage required. Of a truth we face harder problems in staging Shakespeare to-day than were known to the Elizabethans.

When the English people began to take Shakespeare seriously in the early years of the eighteenth century, their tendency was to focus the lights on the leading characters. People went to the theatre to see Betterton and Cibber and Garrick and the rest. This practice of "starring" was at first an unconscious innovation; the intensive study of Shakespeare's great rôles became the history of the British Stage. The old tales were a little distorted in the process, because the chief characters were now endowed by the public with too much importance. The original, plain story-telling purpose of the play was all but forgotten. Such is the natural history of art. It begins by story-telling and it ends in virtuosity. Stendhal said that the most powerful rendering of Shakespeare which he had ever witnessed was done in a barn. If our managers will but remember the humble surroundings to which the children of Shakespeare's wit were born, a great many qualities which are to-day lost in the staging will reappear in the plays.

IX

KING LEAR

THERE is something to be gained by an irresponsible and random flight through Shakespeare. The sublime is inaccessible to study, and Shakespeare's greatest poetry, dealing as it does with minds distraught, with the chaotic emotions of dislocated natures, cannot be understood by a well-ordered and correct attention. We must be dreamy and indifferent as we read "Hamlet." We must accept and relinquish the scenes in "King Lear" without an attempt to understand them. Their meaning will be surrendered to us later by memory, and will live in those regions where the things themselves were born, on the threshold of the unconscious and the incommunicable.

The play "King Lear" has shown that it will survive any treatment. It was fitted with a happy ending by Nahum Tate in Charles the Second's time, and the version held the stage for one hundred and sixty years. In the meantime all the great minds of Europe had had their say about it, and many great actors of Europe had done what human genius could do to interpret it. There grew up, both in Germany and in England, a great public of educated persons, who knew every word of the play by heart, and attended a performance of "King Lear" much as a modern audience attends the performance by some new pianist of one of Beethoven's great sonatas.

In fact the eighteenth and nineteenth centuries did for "Lear," "Hamlet," "Macbeth," "Othello," and "Richard III" what the last half of the nineteenth century did for Beethoven: they produced a special race of prodigious experts, created by the plays and by the music — gladiators of art, who gave exhibitions on a scale undreamed of by Shakespeare or Beethoven, and produced effects that would have startled the creators. Beethoven was, no doubt, a musical person, and he was by profession a pianist; but if Beethoven were to play one of his concertos before a modern audience, which knew every interpretation that the work has undergone since the times of Liszt and Rubenstein, he would cut a sorry figure. The size of the instrument, the size of the auditorium, and the expectations of the public would crush him.

The exploitation of Shakespeare as a field for starring came to a climax first in Garrick and next in Edmund Kean, who, to judge by all accounts, was the greatest of English actors, and became to the British stage what Rachel was to the French stage, the messiah of an epoch when people went to the theatre, not to see a play, but to see an actor. By the sacrifice of all other interests to this one interest certain effects were produced which will not soon be repeated. They imply that the whole passion of an age is bent toward representing with virtuosity something that has been created, schemed, and brought to a focus by former genius. At such epochs the actor is classed by the public as almost the poet's equal.

I transcribe a few critiques on Edmund Kean

from the treasure-house out of which most of my learning is drawn — Mr. Furness's edition: —

It has been said that "Lear" was a study for anyone who would make himself acquainted with the workings of an insane mind. There is no doubt of it. And it is no less true that Mr. Kean was a perfect exemplification of it. His eye, when his senses are first forsaking him, giving a questioning look at what he saw, as if all before him was undergoing a strange and bewildering change which confused his brain — the wandering, lost motions of his hands, which seemed feeling for something familiar to them, on which they might take hold, and be assured of a safe reality — the under monotone of his voice, as if he was questioning his own being, and all which surrounded him — the continuous, but slight oscillating motion of the body, — all expressed, with fearful truth, the dreamy state of a mind fast unsettling, and making vain and weak efforts to find its way back to its wonted reason. There was a childish, feeble gladness in the eye, and a half-piteous smile about the mouth at times, which one could scarce look upon without shedding tears. As the derangement increased upon him, his eye lost its notice of what surrounded him, wandering over everything as if he saw it not, and fastening upon the creatures of his crazed brain. The helpless and dignified fondness with which he clings to Edgar as an insane brother is another instance of the justness of Mr. Kean's conceptions. Nor does he lose the air of insanity even in the fine moralizing parts, and where he inveighs against the corruptions of the world. There is a madness even in his reason. . . .

Since his first appearance at Drury Lane he had never lost an opportunity of improving his attainment in "Lear"; so anxious was he to impart truth and natural coloring to his performance that, in order to observe the details and manifestations of real insanity, he constantly visited St. Luke's and Bethlehem hospitals ere he appeared in the old King; and, tranquilly relying upon the unfailing fertility of his intellectual resources, he anticipated this effort as the last seal of his theatrical renown. He knew that, when he came to the trial, his mind would be thoroughly imbued with the properties of the character; and, fearless as to the result, he quietly said that he would make the audience as mad as he himself should be. . . .

Who that once heard can ever forget the terrors of that terrific curse, where, in the wild storm of his conflicting passions, he threw himself on his knees, "lifted up his arms, like withered stumps, threw his head quite back and, in that position, as if severed from all that held him to society, breathed a heart-struck prayer, like the figure of a man obtruncated"? . . .

The next scene is the finish of the whole performance, and certainly it is the noblest execution of lofty genius that the modern stage has ever witnessed — always excepting the same actor's closing scene in the Third Act of "Othello." It is impossible for words to convey anything like an adequate description of the extraordinary acting in the whole of this scene — of the electrical effect produced from the transition from "Bid 'em come forth and hear me," etc., to "O, are you come?" — the mingled suspicion and tenderness with which he tells Regan of Goneril's treatment of him; the exquisite tone of pathos thrown into the mock petition to Regan, "I confess that I am old," etc.; the wonderful depth and nobility of expression given to the ironical speech to Goneril, "I did not bid the thunder-bearer strike," etc.; the pure and touching simplicity of "I gave you all"; and lastly, the splendid close of this scene with the speech, "Heavens, drop your patience down," etc., in which the bitter delight of anticipated revenge, and the unbending sense of habitual dignity, contend against the throes and agonies of a torn and bursting heart.

After such a series of heroic actors as Garrick, Kemble, Kean, Booth, and Salvini, the kaleidoscope of time must fall into new shapes before other aspects of Shakespeare can reveal themselves. It will not be till some years after the death of Josef Hoffman and our other titanic pianists, that humanity will dare creep toward a new understanding of Beethoven. Yet time passes, manners change. We can never be sure that we ourselves should have liked Garrick's Hamlet, or have been carried away by Paganini. I have seen Edwin Booth and Salvini, who were the latest stars in the slowly setting galaxy — or, as it were, dynasty — of great tragedians; and I am going to confess that in "King Lear," though each was extraordinary, there did not seem to be mists and clouds enough about the old King. The mind's theatre was too bare; Lear had slipped his envelope and was too isolated, too visible, too articulate, too cunningly lighted. I believe that this effect was due, not, as Charles Lamb would have it, to Shakespeare's unfitness for the stage, but to the neglect by modern stage managers of the minor plots and minor characters in the drama.

It was long ago discovered that two very similar legends are woven together in this play — the story of Lear, and a tale about an old man and his two sons which Shakespeare probably ran across in Sidney's "Arcadia." Why were these two stories combined?

The mystery of "King Lear" lies in the strange sheaf of things that Shakespeare grasped in his hand before he began to write the play. It was to be a tragedy — that is to say, a great many of the characters were to be killed. Eleven of them are killed, only the colorless Albany being left alive — Albany who has hardly a cue at all during the evening. The plot was to be about King Lear and his wicked daughters. King Lear was to be driven forth in a storm, to go mad, and die. But this theme was not large enough for Shakespeare. His instinct for quantity and for reduplications had led him in "Hamlet" to reinforce the equivocal madness of Hamlet with the real madness of Ophelia. In "Richard III," he had multiplied curses and ghosts. Such devices support each other dramatically. In "King Lear" he pursues the bold plan of having the whole tragedy of filial ingratitude toward Lear shadowed by a second tragedy of filial ingratitude toward another old man, Gloucester. This second old man must not only have one good son and one bad son, but he must be blinded, thrust out alone into the countryside, and bidden to smell his way to Dover, so that he may become a pendant to Lear.

Lear is to go mad: therefore there must be other mad persons, or pretended mad persons, or irresponsible persons, to support Lear's madness. A mad person surrounded by sane persons on the stage is lonely. In a good tragedy the terrors and curses and general hellward tendency of things must affect as many minds and persons as possible. Thus when the old man, Gloucester, goes out with a torch to rescue the King in the storm, he says, in the presence of the really mad King, and of the pretended mad Edgar, and of the Fool, that he is almost mad himself, — "grief has crazed his wits" — the remark applies to almost everyone on the stage.

All these mad people are good people. And there

is to be another good man, Kent, a faithful follower of Lear whom Shakespeare brings in in disguise. Therefore there must be more disguises, and Edgar is introduced in five different ones. As a character in disguise Edgar supports Kent; as the good son of an unjust parent, he supports Cordelia; as a pretended madman, he supports the King and the Fool. Note that Cordelia, Kent, the Fool, Edgar, and old Gloucester are all in sympathy with the King, and all are involved with the King in one brainstorm, or, as someone has called it, in the "globose of whirling passion." For fear that even this battalion of sympathetic characters will not suffice as a sounding-board to Lear, Shakespeare has thrown in a description of a sympathetic Gentleman, who heralds the entry of Lear in the storm, and gives us a picture of the old man running unbonneted and bidding what will take all. It is to this bushel-basket instinct of Shakespeare's that we owe the unique and tremendous power of "Lear"; and seem to watch (as Hudson said) "a handful of tumult enbosomed in a sea, gradually overspreading, pervading, and convulsing the entire mass." Let us return to the list of characters.

In a tragedy there must be some wicked people. The bad daughters of the Lear legend supply two of them, and they are exactly alike. Lear is first cut to the heart by one daughter, then by the next. The critics have tried to distinguish their rôles, but it cannot be done. Goneril and Regan are mere names, which allow Shakespeare to double his instrument.

Two other wicked people are provided, — as

wicked as possible, — in the nursery-tale manner; namely, Edmund and Cornwall. They assist in persecuting the two good old men, Lear and Gloucester; and they do it in the crudest manner, as understudies.

But a tragedy also needs a chorus, a moralist, a commentator, a Melancholy Jaques, Shakespeare himself — the Fool.

If I had not been told so often that the theme of Shakespeare's "Lear" was filial ingratitude, I should have said that the theme was houseless poverty, and "blessed are the poor in spirit." All the good people in the play are obsessed with the idea of the sacredness of beggars. The greatest scenes of the play stage this idea. The talk about poverty begins immediately after the King's abdication. Almost the first words that Kent says to Lear are: —

Kent. A very honest-hearted fellow, and as poor as the King.

Lear. If thou be as poor for a subject as he is for a King, thou art poor enough.

Now it is out of character for Lear to say this; but as the point must be made, and there is no one else on the stage to make it, Shakespeare gives the cue to Lear. (It makes less difference *who* says a thing on the stage than most people will believe.)

The Fool soon rings the changes on the thought of poverty, and Kent, when in the stocks, says "nothing almost sees miracles, but poverty." Immediately after this Edgar, being alone on the stage, gives his monody on Poverty: —

I heard myself proclaimed;
And by the happy hollow of a tree
Escaped the hunt.

. . . .

I will preserve myself: and am bethought
To take the basest and most poorest shape
That ever penury in contempt of man
Brought near to beast: my face I 'll grime with filth,
Blanket my loins, elf all my hair in knots,
And with presented nakedness out-face
The winds and persecutions of the sky.
The country gives me proof and precedent
Of Bedlam beggars, who with roaring voices
Strike in their numbed and mortified bare arms
Pins, wooden pricks, nails, sprigs of rosemary;
And with this horrible object, from low farms,
Poor pelting villages, sheep-cotes and mills,
Sometime with lunatic bans, sometime with prayers
Enforce their charity.

The thought of poverty again flits by in Lear's

O reason not the need: our basest beggars
Are in their poorest things superfluous:
Allow not nature more than nature needs,
Man's life 's as cheap as beast's: thou art a lady;
If only to go warm were gorgeous,
Why, nature needs not what thou gorgeous wear'st,
Which scarcely keeps thee warm.

The King is still thinking about the poor, as he allows the Fool to lead him to the hovel:—

LEAR. Come on, my boy: how dost, my boy? art cold?
I am cold myself. Where is this straw, my fellow?
The art of our necessities is strange,

That can make vile things precious. Come, your
hovel.

The theme comes in with trumpets in the scene before the hovel.

Poor naked wretches, wheresoe'er you are,
That bide the pelting of this pitiless storm,
How shall your houseless heads and unfed sides,
Your loop'd and window'd raggedness, defend you
From seasons such as these? O, I have ta'en
Too little care of this! Take physic, pomp;
Expose thyself to feel what wretches feel,
That thou mayst shake the superflux to them
And show the heavens more just.

Lear is so obsessed by the thought of poverty, that at the sight of Edgar he tries to tear off his own clothes.

LEAR. Why, thou wert better in thy grave than to answer with thy uncovered body this extremity of the skies. Is man no more than this? Consider him well. Thou owest the worm no silk, the beast no hide, the sheep no wool, the cat no perfume. Ha! here 's three on 's are sophisticated. Thou art the thing itself: unaccommodated man is no more but such a poor, bare, forked animal as thou art. Off, off, you lendings! come, unbutton here.
(*Tearing off his clothes*)

The theme is given out again by Gloucester, in words which are all but a repetition of Lear's, and are an expansion of Kent's remark in the stocks: —

GLOU. That I am wretched
Makes thee the happier. Heavens, deal so still!
Let the superfluous and lust-dieted man,
That slaves your ordinance, that will not see

> Because he doth not feel, feel your power quickly;
> So distribution should undo excess
> And each man have enough.

And Edgar says the same thing again in the fields near Dover when, in the disguise of a peasant, he meets his father.

> GLOU. Now, good sir, what are you?
> EDGAR. A most poor man, made tame to fortune's blows;
> Who, by the art of known and feeling sorrows,
> Am pregnant to good pity.

Observe that all these sentiments are perfectly natural in the mouths of all these characters, because of the antiphonal basis on which the whole play is set up. The inner structure of "King Lear," and the reinforcements of character by character, and effect by effect, are what make it the greatest of Shakespeare's tragedies.

The power of iteration on the stage was never better illustrated. Every speech strikes in the same spot on the same musical anvil. Before Lear actually goes mad, he prophesies eight times, in *crescendo*, that he is about to go mad. Perhaps the true resemblance between Shakespeare's tragedies and Greek tragedy is to be found in this passion of Shakespeare for converging repetitions of thought.

In producing this play, its inner structure must be borne in mind. Unless the underplots and minor characters are staged in an interesting way, the play will lose half its power; for it is upon the strings of these half-heard instruments that the resonance of the whole depends. The entire text cannot be given, it is too long: the problem is to keep the tale moving by using the vital parts of it. Much costume, much scenery, or a too elaborate storm, will kill the drama. We should accept the conventions of a crude symbolism, and patch together the scenes with a free Elizabethan hand, so that a child or an ignorant person can follow the story.

Shakespeare often uses a change of scene as we to-day use a drop curtain — merely to break in upon a long interview, and give variety.

Thus, the scene where Kent is in the stocks is divided by the apparition of Edgar on the heath. The madness of Lear in the hovel scene is separated from his madness at the farmhouse by a short and very dull interview between the two villains, Edmund and Cornwall.

The whole of this play, after the opening pageant of the abdication, is a medley of detached scenes: it is in form a scatterbrained play, and in substance the most solid thing in human drama.

One more kind of iteration in it must be noticed. Part of the pathos in "Lear" comes from the way in which the old gentleman is haled about from one place to another.

We see him first refused admittance at Albany's palace; then thrust out in the storm from Gloucester's palace; then on the heath in the storm; then before a hovel in the storm; then rescued by Gloucester and taken to a farmhouse in the storm; next, removed on a pallet from the farmhouse; next, wandering in the fields near Dover; next, on a bed, asleep in a tent in the French camp; then being led by soldiers across the stage, in company with Cordelia, to find a place of safety; then brought on the stage in company with Cordelia, both of them as prisoners; next, led off the stage, guarded; and finally, reëntering, with the dead body of Cordelia in his arms.

We must deal with the stage business in "Lear" with as light a hand as if it were a farce, and the tragedy in it will take care of itself.

X

MACBETH

THERE are so many reasons why Shakespeare's greater plays affect us powerfully, that it seems like fatuity to point out special good qualities in any one of them; yet, as a great many people have tried their hand at this, and the practice never seems to have injured the plays, I will hazard a few remarks upon the nature of dramatic writing, and illustrate them with the play of "Macbeth."

The main point about dramatic writing is that everything must be made obvious. A man who writes a book may state his idea and develop it and adorn it at leisure. He may even hide it with charms, and compensate the reader in a hundred ways for his obscurity. But in a theatre ideas must be delivered through a series of shocks. Shakespeare's method of doing this is by the contrast of opposites. He places two effects beside one another, and causes the idea to jump out by the contact. This is true as to his great effects of element with element, conception with conception, scene with scene. It is true also of his dramatis personæ. He must have kings and beggars, good angels and devils. It is true also of the give-and-take of his dialogue. The dazzling play of opposites throughout Shakespeare, whether in adjectives, phrases, scenes, characters, or climaxes, is what makes him stageable. Say "Heaven" to him, he says "Hell"; "Black," — "White"; "To be," — "Not to be." He shadows each impression with a double that has been refracted from the thing itself, and causes an idea to stand in the air vividly, like an apparition.

This double-flash in Shakespeare is to be found in his earliest and in his latest work. There is a famous *emendation* of his text which shows up this action of his mind in a startling manner. In "Love 's Labor's Lost" the professed love-hater, Biron, gives a whimsical description of Cupid, calling him "a wimpled, whining, purblind, wayward boy," "a regent of love-rhymes, lord of folded arms," etc. One of the lines in the folio text reads as follows: —

> This signior Iunio's giant dwarf don Cupid.

After the commentators had wearied themselves with trying to identify "Iunio," or "Junio," with one Junius, a Roman captain in a play by Beaumont and Fletcher; after they had amended "Junio" to "Julio" and had imagined a reference to Giulio Romano — someone at last suggested the reading, —

> This senior-junior, giant-dwarf, Dan Cupid, —

and learned and unlearned alike shouted "Shakespeare!"

I mention in passing this passion of Shakespeare for the antithetical. It is his habit, a part of his dramatic technique, and it runs all through his work. But we must not fix our attention on it, or try to fathom it; for many shimmers of fancy are at play, some of them small and silvery as aspen leaves, and others as large as the shadow cast by a mainsail.

He sometimes enhances a great effect of gorgeous eloquence by placing in front of it a bank of gloomy foreboding and quiet talk. He does this in "Henry V," where he introduces Henry's magnificent poetry about the responsibility of kings with a dark, muttering, introspective scene in prose — a sort of antechamber to Apollo's temple. In "Macbeth" there is a notable case of great blanket-work, or heavy cloud-rolling and premonitory muffled gloom, almost of stupidity. Between the witch-and-murder beginnings of the play and the battle-scenes at the end of it, there falls a long scene at the English court, which is one of the dullest scenes in Shakespeare (Act IV, Sc. 3). Malcolm and Macduff are discovered: they declare that they will seek out some desolate shade and weep their sad bosoms empty. Both the characters seem to be half asleep, and to be talking about their dreams. Nothing could rest us better from the murders we have just been witnessing, or better set off the turmoil in Scotland that is to follow immediately, than the stupor of this scene.

It is idle to inquire how far Shakespeare was conscious of his lights and shades, of his contrasted settings and antithetical characters. Falstaff is a fat old man, the Prince, a thin young man; Caliban balances Ariel; Malvolio is a prig, Toby Belch, a scapegrace. Such types appeared to him in pairs and are somehow parts of each other. So also in a single character there are often contrasts that give it brilliancy; for example, the wisdom of fools, the fierceness of the gentle, the jests of gravediggers, the pomposity of the empty-minded. It is always a hiatus that makes us laugh or cry on the stage.

MACBETH

In "Hamlet" the drama arises, as we have seen, out of the heart-piercing emergency-calls of fate, and Hamlet's heartrending incapacity to meet them.

In "Macbeth" the contrasts are gigantic and Rembrandtesque. The drama is an old-fashioned, blood-and-thunder, boys' play, and its merit lies in the way it is done. The terror it inspires is due to the abyss that lies between the inner natures of Macbeth and Lady Macbeth, and the murder which they perpetrate. Recite the facts of the play as if done by the kind of persons who usually do such deeds, and the story will have little interest. It would be a foolish task for us to prove that such sensitive, high-keyed, metaphysical natures as Macbeth and Lady Macbeth — persons who tremble at shadows and are haunted by nightmares — seldom commit murders — as foolish as proving that the practical, hardened villains of the world do not discourse wittily and gayly, and enjoy the drama of their own existence as Richard III and Iago seem to do. Such characters are dramatic devices; and we must accept the hypersensitiveness of Macbeth and Lady Macbeth as one of Shakespeare's greatest strokes of genius.

When Macbeth first comes on the stage, he is already unhinged, because the thought of murder has been flitting through his head. His wife and he have lived so long together that they are exactly in tune with one another. It makes no difference which of them first had the idea of a murder, for together they make up the picture of the terrified person. In their conversations they often exchange rôles, now one of them taking the lead, and now the other. Although it has been customary since Mrs. Siddons's time to regard Lady Macbeth as the worse criminal of the two, there is really little to choose between them, and Macbeth plots the murder of Banquo without confiding in his wife. To my mind they appear as a single dramatic element. Lady Macbeth actually dies of remorse and mental trouble, while Macbeth, although he has a fighting rôle to distract his mind, gibbers with metaphysical terrors till the end. He identifies the sickness of Lady Macbeth with his own remorse, and says to the doctor, in regard to Lady Macbeth's "thick coming fancies," —

> Cure her of that.
> Canst thou not minister to a mind diseased,
> Pluck from the memory a rooted sorrow,
> Raze out the written troubles of the brain,
> And with some sweet oblivious antidote
> Cleanse the stuff'd bosom of that perilous stuff
> Which weighs upon the heart?

Even at his final meeting with Macduff, he is obsessed by the witches and their prophecies: he is living the inner life of terror and remorse.

> Accursed be that tongue that tells me so,
> For it hath cow'd my better part of man!
> And be these juggling fiends no more believ'd,
> That palter with us in a double sense;
> That keep the word of promise to our ear,
> And break it to our hope.

Thus, only two minutes before he is killed, Macbeth is seen reviewing the story of their crime, just as his wife reviews that story in her sleep-walking.

In "Macbeth," Shakespeare appears to have doubled his leading character, just as he doubled his whole plot in "King Lear."

Let us glance rapidly through the play and recall its fierce lights and black shadows, its plunges from mood to mood, from crashing tempest to ominous and horrible spots of calm. The witches in the opening are almost pure allegory. Macbeth doubts whether he has really seen them or not, and we ourselves see them as portions of his mood. Then comes Lady Macbeth with the letter, and we see that both she and her lord are in the coils of an obsession. They are both frightfully excited. The look on Macbeth's face confirms his wife's doubt as to his capacity. Both of them are, from the beginning, very much afraid that they will be found out. Murder is a business foreign to their natures, and they know that they will do it bunglingly. The unsuspecting Duncan and his train enter immediately, and a wafture of æolian music accompanies his step on the threshold of the rude, bleak, forbidding Scotch castle from which he is never to emerge alive.

BANQUO. This guest of summer,
The temple-haunting martlet, does approve
By his loved mansionry that the heaven's breath
Smells wooingly here: no jutty, frieze,
Buttress, nor coign of vantage, but this bird
Hath made his pendent bed and procreant cradle:
Where they most breed and haunt, I have observ'd
The air is delicate.

Surely this is a dramatic introduction to a coarse, feudal, uncomfortable, gloomy, and bare-walled piece of butchery.

I shall not recite the murder itself. The physical blood and grime of the thing is as awful to the gentle natures of Macbeth and his wife as is the horror of the crime itself, and the terror, always present, of being discovered.

After the realism of the truly dreadful and most lifelike scenes between Macbeth and his wife during the murder, they stand shivering, and ask what o'clock it is, and listen for the owl and the cricket.

The audience at this point receives a shock as of blank emptiness. Everything has stopped: we see the very boards of the stage. Then, as if from another world, comes the knocking of the porter, — daylight, — and the noisy, innocent, leisurely obscenity of the porter.

This plunge from the imaginative terrors of midnight into the cruel facts of common day is perhaps the most sudden transition in drama. It is the daylight that makes the murder so ghastly in review; and it is the natural goodness of Macbeth and of his lady, their domestic quality, their spiritual remoteness from the thing in hand, that makes us shudder.

Of all the horror-breeding passages in the drama, the most telling are the two speeches that give us a glimpse into Macbeth as a poetic, introspective, soulful person. At the very moment when he is encouraging himself and lashing himself up to be as bloody as possible there comes to him a vision of the quiet life.

We have scotch'd the snake, not kill'd it:
She 'll close and be herself.

. . . .

Better be with the dead,
Whom we, to gain our peace, have sent to peace,
Than on the torture of the mind to lie
In restless ecstasy. Duncan is in his grave;
After life's fitful fever he sleeps well;
Treason has done his worst: nor steel, nor poison,
Malice domestic, foreign levy, nothing,
Can touch him further.

Again when the servant announces that the English forces are upon him, Macbeth is seized with an access of sentiment — a vision of lost happiness.

SERVANT. The English force, so please you.
MACBETH. Take thy face hence.
Seyton! — I am sick at heart,
When I behold — Seyton, I say! — This push
Will cheer me ever, or disseat me now.
I have liv'd long enough: my way of life
Is fall'n into the sere, the yellow leaf,
And that which should accompany old age,
As honor, love, obedience, troops of friends,
I must not look to have; but, in their stead,
Curses, not loud but deep, mouth-honor, breath,
Which the poor heart would fain deny, and dare not.
Seyton!

To no other dramatist but Shakespeare did nature reveal these climaxes of antiphonal feeling — a devil rushing in where a god is called, or *vice versa*.

XI

THE COMEDIES

In the days when the Germans were marching on Paris, and from time to time thereafter, whenever there seemed to be a chance that the Germans might win the war, I was haunted by momentary visions of the past, — that part of the past whose spirit was threatened, — the spirit of joy, relaxation, and dreamy happiness. I saw, as in a flash, Falstaff sitting on the tavern bench in the sun and unbuttoning his belt after dinner, Toby Belch going to burn more sack and swearing it was not late yet. I heard Bottom calling for an almanac, and boasting that he would do it in 'Ercles' vein, Audrey asking Touchstone, "What is honest? Is it a good thing?" and Grumio describing his master's wedding-journey with the Shrew.

Such scenes from Shakespeare, and fragmentary memories of the man himself and of his age, would pass by in my mind as if they were the thing attacked by this whole German onslaught: and, indeed, they were the citadel; they, to the German mind, were the enemy that must be razed out of the world's life if Kaiserdom were to exist at all. There was, of course, always a possibility that the Germans would win, and that an era of darkness and violence would follow which should make the little English paradise of freedom, out of which Shakespeare's comedies had risen, seem even more of a miracle than it had seemed before.

This war-experience gave me a new clue to English literature. A sense of personal safety is one of the elements that is felt all through English letters. It is the climate in which the English genius, which is the genius for happiness, developed. How similar in spirit is all the joyous part of English fiction, from Chaucer to Surtees's sporting books! There is the same glow in "Twelfth Night" that there is in "Pickwick Papers." The rapture of mere existence is in all this work. It has been made without intention. Intention is a damage to it, as we see often in Dickens, and always in George Eliot; and the substratum of it is common life, good-humor, observation, courage, an indeterminate way of living, and an abundance of force. The English write as they live — in the moment.

The earlier British humorists set the pace for the later ones; and, as it happened, the social system of England changed so little during eight centuries, and so much of the Middle Ages survived in it, that the types and situations, the high life and the low life of the land, the nobles and the ostlers, the Hotspurs, Dogberrys, grooms, murderers, and Sam Wellers have afforded a continuous family of picturesque characters and grotesque contrasts, which have been reflected in the humorous fiction of each new age, under the guidance of tradition, and by the light of the great masters of the earlier times.

Ever since Shakespeare's day, his hand is to be seen everywhere in the fiction and humor of England. It is in Fielding, in Smollett and Scott; in Dickens, Thackeray, and Trollope. They are gay people, the English, and except when they try to be clever, are the cleverest people in the world. Ebulliency, enthusiasm, and the absence of literary pose are the great features of English literature. If you cast your eye over the whole panorama, the low life in it appears to be better done than the high life. The reason of this may be that great writers are almost always men of the people; and, as they thoroughly know the people, they describe them to the life; but they make guesses as to the aristocracy.

In Shakespeare, both the high life and the low life are equally convincing when we read the plays to ourselves; but on the modern stage a very strange thing happens: the low comedy is apt to be heavy and conscientious. It may be that the Puritan Revolution made such a break in the old Gothic horse-play and comic tradition, that the art of it was lost. These thoughts occurred to me while watching a rather second-rate performance of "Twelfth Night" in French. It was an absurd exhibition in some ways. The costumes were burlesque; Malvolio was schematized, understood and presented as a serious type, the part being acted so conscientiously that Malvolio became a bore. On the other hand the buffoonery was gay. I was su prised to see gay buffoonery in a Shakespearean performance; and quite suddenly it occurred to me that this was right, this was the way that Shakespeare's droll parts should be played. There is a technique about buffoonery, and the clowns of Molière, in whose antics the old mediæval tomfoolery has come down to us, throw light on Shakespeare's low comedy.

As for high comedy, Garrick used to say that in tragedy he could always bring down the house, no matter in what mood he stepped upon the boards, whether he had a headache or felt sick or indifferent. "But comedy — comedy is a serious business!" This is no doubt a universal experience with actors; and Shakespeare's comedies, each of which is so different in spirit, in tempo, in coloring from the rest, are probably the most difficult of all comedies to act well. "As You Like It," for instance, is a water-color sketch — there is little drama in it. Rosalind's repartees cannot be gilded. Touchstone's soliloquies will not bear a frame. The set speeches in "As You Like It" — as for instance, "Now, my co-mates and brothers-in-exile," or Oliver's two long speeches describing how he was rescued by his brothers from the sucked and hungry lioness — cannot be informed with passion; and yet they must be beautiful. They say that Mozart's music is the most difficult of all music to play — it is so perfect and yet so delicate. You must live yourself back into the world as it was before the French Revolution if you would play Mozart correctly. No one has the time to do this, and therefore Mozart cannot be played. In like manner, "As You Like It" is apt to drag. We have all become heavy-fisted nowadays, and we pound our texts. Where poetry, foolery, and philosophy meet, as they do in these sylvan scenes, — all of them tinged with a world that has long ago disappeared, — we are like burglars dancing a minuet. Perhaps, instead of bewailing the vanishment of the old English stage, we ought rather to wonder at the genius of Shakespeare, which has so long kept alive the art of imaginative, happy badinage, during a century whose social life has been growing ever more and more unimaginative, graceless, and practical.

In giving one of the lesser comedies, the mood of the piece is harder to find, and its keynote harder to sound, than in the great ones. The "Merchant of Venice" expounds itself like a tragedy, and is so various, interesting, and full of passion that it is easy to act. The lighter plays present the heavier problems. In "Much Ado About Nothing" the plot is more serious and the whole humor and intrigue of the piece more sprightly than in "As You Like It." How shall we find, how hit upon that talisman, that "Open, Sesame," which shall show the inner life of each of these delicate masterpieces? The plays themselves must teach us. They were not created, nor have they been sustained, by any academy. We have only tradition, personal feeling, and experience to guide us.

The "Taming of the Shrew" has still another, and very different, temperament of its own. It is a very subtle, quizzical, humane, philosophic piece of nonsense. In the "Midsummer Night's Dream" you have, again, a region of fancy so utterly different from all these last-mentioned plays, that it seems as if it must have been made by another hand. It is steeped in the peculiar atmosphere of the world's fairyland, and seems to be a whole literature in itself. "Twelfth Night" is, again, a new universe. It is the best light comedy in the world and swims like a ruddy planet, bearing the inhabitants of the Golden Age. It is a saturnalia of good feeling, leisure, wit, and amusement in which both high and low revel by day and night. Each of these comedies is a unity, and resounds harmoniously when its chords are touched; but the works must not be attacked with vigor, and the keynotes of them must be rather listened for and imagined than struck.

Perhaps the sophisticated modern person can best approach Shakespeare's comedies by thinking of them as child's plays, things beneath his serious notice and therefore to be humored. Otherwise the casket scene in the "Merchant of Venice" will disgust him. It is, indeed, probable that the folk-lore and fairy tales of the world are kept alive by the infant population of the world, and that no man, who first discovers these things after he is grown up, will be apt to find much meaning in them. The ancients lived on nursery tales; but every man, even then, had learned these tales first in the nursery. And I suspect that to-day, if the myths and auld wives' stories should die out of our nurseries, they would die out altogether; and then, of course, there would be nothing for the learned to talk about except politics, economics, eugenics, and ethnology — subjects which deal with mankind in masses, and take the individual for granted. To the poet there are no Masses, but only men. He speaks to each one of us severally. The poets throw open the windows and let in currents that carry life, awaken energy, and make men sensitive, powerful, wise, eloquent, capable of seeing the world, — I will not say as it is, for no man has seen that, — but more nearly as it is than men ever can see it without the light of poetry.

XII

SHAKESPEARE'S TYPES

SHAKESPEARE'S gentleness toward the evil in human nature is his rarest quality. We seem to find in every line of him a sentiment which he has put, strangely enough, in the mouth of Henry V.

> There is a soul of goodness in things evil
> Would men observingly distill it out.

He can hardly bear to draw a villain. In some cases, where the plot calls for a villain, as in "Hamlet," "The Tempest," or the "Merchant of Venice," — cases in which any other playwright would have given us wickedness, — Shakespeare draws a weak or unfortunate character. In "Hamlet" the wicked King is half repentant. In the "Merchant of Venice" Shylock is a much-injured and very human person. In the "Tempest" Caliban is convincingly good and unconvincingly bad, a rudimentary half-soul. Prospero, to be sure, considers the creature ungrateful; but *we* do not think him ungrateful, we think of him as a creature who has never had half a chance, and we almost love him.

In "Romeo and Juliet" Shakespeare manages to get on without a villain. In "As You Like It" we have, as the bad man in the piece, a faint, obliterated personality, Orlando's elder brother, and we have also the usurping Duke: both of them should, of course, be villains; but they both repent, and were never truly bad anyway. In "Much Ado About Nothing" there is a Don John, who is a mild discontented bastard — not a bad fellow, but a failure, and one who feels that he is down and out. Shakespeare thinks that men in this situation become villains, to ease their minds. When Don John is told by a pal about the intended marriage of Hero, he says, "Will it serve for any model to build mischief on?" and proceeds to make much ado. It amounts almost to trifling with an audience, to pass off such a duffer as Don John for a villain. In "Measure for Measure" there was a chance for a really bad man in the wicked old judge, Angelo, who proposes the infamous bargain to Isabella by which her brother is to be released. But Angelo is a lay figure: he has no reality. Shakespeare does n't even try to make Angelo's passion real, and perhaps he could n't have made it convincing; because Shakespeare did n't understand bad people. In the early poem of "Lucrece" his treatment of Tarquin foreshadows his later treatment of Macbeth; for Tarquin is represented as a highly sensitive and metaphysical person who, before his deed, is horrified at the thought of it, and the instant he has done the deed, sounds the doom against himself.

In a general way it may be said that Shakespeare's villains are either sympathetically presented as men with much good in them, or else they are, not gods out of a machine, but devils out of a machine — toys of stage-land.

The only characters I can think of in Shakespeare who give one a shudder as being both very wicked and very real, are Goneril and Regan; and they are women. It seems to be a fact in nature that women may be saints or may be demons, but that men are on the whole good-hearted, fumbling, stumbling creatures, never perfect, and never entirely bad. A woman may be entirely wicked; and if Iago's rôle had been cast for a feminine part, we should have had the most terrific thing in literature.

Shakespeare reserves all his adoration for his heroines. His good women are angelic beings. His young heroines, Miranda, Cordelia, Imogen, Juliet, Perdita seem all to be spirits of the same heaven, and are like different aspects of the same woman rather than different women: they are the quintessence of romanticism. His heroines of mature years, as for instance, Hermione (in "A Winter's Tale"), and Queen Katherine, have the same quality. He cannot refrain from throwing a dash of connubial romance into Cleopatra.

He uses his men as foils to set off his heroines. But alas for the men! He can no more draw a hero, than he can draw a villain. Romeo, Hamlet, Orlando, Ferdinand (in the "Tempest"), Posthumus (in "Cymbeline"), Claudio (in "Much Ado"), Bertram (in "All 's Well"), Claudio (in "Measure for Measure") — what an array of unheroic youths! Shakespeare produces good stupid men at will — Horatio (in "Hamlet"), Antonio (in the "Merchant of Venice"), Brutus, Coriolanus, Malcolm (in "Macbeth"). They are foils to the women. Thus it would appear that the greatest dramatist of the world has not drawn a single satisfactory hero. The nearest Shakespeare comes to a hero is in Julius Cæsar, whose few cues somehow give us a tremendous impression of the heroic. Had it been necessary for dramatic effect, Shakespeare would have given us heroes; but his mind ran on pathetic climaxes, which are the making of heroines and the marring of heroes.

Another consequence of Shakespeare's natal benignity was that he could not be cynical. Now and then he has occasion to try. The plot of the "Taming of the Shrew" gave him an opportunity for cynicism; but Shakespeare burlies it over into good-humor: he keeps the plot farcical, boisterous, and fanciful. Petruchio is a sound-hearted man, and is really very fond of Katherine.

On several occasions, however, Shakespeare tried to write a really cynical play, and in such cases he always produced a bad play. For instance, a true cynic would have written a good play about Timon or Troilus. Shakespeare did not know that pessimism constitutes a field of art by itself. Pessimism is not a mood that a man can drop into, and then do something clever, which will compete with the work of the professionals. Pessimism is a serious business: to be a good pessimist requires lifelong study. A man must have been morbid in his youth, sick perhaps, unjustly thwarted, clever, and misunderstood. He must, before reaching the age of seventeen, have cried out, "Darkness be thou my light!" and proceeded to live in shadows, to luxuriate in depression and despair.

The greatest pessimist who ever lived was Leopardi, who complained that the reading of Byron destroyed his gift. It appears that Byron was such a milk-and-water fellow compared to him, that

Leopardi felt his divine powers of pessimism (*il mio pessimismo*) desert him when he read the verses of the pseudo-pessimist: he could not even get up a good fit of rancor in which to denounce the impostor.

We must agree that Byron, in spite of his early training, is an amateur pessimist compared to the continental practitioners. The English are too cheery, too healthy, and live too much in the open air, to be true pessimists. And Shakespeare was the most cheery, healthy, and open-air Englishman of them all. Such a man would never even have dreamed of writing up a cynical theme, unless he happened to be out of sorts, sick perhaps, cross, or not himself. And Shakespeare, with all the genius and all the sincere, passionate acrimony which he displays in "Timon" and in "Troilus," has done no more than exhibit the nervous depression of an optimist — a sort of peevishness, very different from the logic, the cruelty, and the perverse beauty of true cynicism.

Let us lay aside speculation and open the plays at random. Shylock, Hotspur, Falstaff, Mercutio, Polonius, Caliban, Bottom, Petruchio, Toby Belch, have the grotesque, homely vitality of mediæval art. How did these characters come into being? They start from their frames, and seem to exist apart from their context. Yet it is to the context that they owe their existence. In Shakespeare's non-dramatic poetry you do not find any trace of this peculiar power to draw character. In his Sonnets and poems he gives no inkling that such figures would come at his call from the abysses of his imagination. It was the pressure of drama that evoked them. In the

Sonnets we see Shakespeare as a perfectly charming and rather helpless person, with an extreme and even angelic sweetness of disposition, musical rather than witty, and at moments as a half-godlike Orpheus in his gift of song. The "Lucrece" and the "Venus and Adonis" reveal him as an amazingly talented, luxurious, and somewhat artificial court poet. They are decorations for a Borgia palace. The influence of patronage is to be felt in the two longer poems; and if Shakespeare had been born ten years earlier, and had come up to London at the time when the stage was not in condition to absorb his dramatic talents, he would have written metrical romances that would have out-Spensered Spenser. We should have had more court fairylands. But once in harness at the theatre, a kind of good sense, or indifference, or love of his freedom, kept him at his treadmill of play-writing. It turned out that he could write, or learned to write, *any* kind of poetry that a situation called for. His characters are by-products — as it were, discoveries. He puts the story into the crucible of his mind and the characters are the result. The "Merry Wives of Windsor" is a play not founded on a tale or a piece of history that touched Shakespeare's fancy; but is a thing manufactured to order; therefore it contains no Dogberry, no Toby Belch, no Touchstone. Unless Shakespeare's interest was excited by a story, his powers were not awakened.

It is very remarkable that Shakespeare never developed a consistent technique, but to the end of his life was always at the mercy of his theme. "Romeo and Juliet" is one of the earliest of his plays and one of the best. His greatest tragedies were written in alternate years with his very worst plays. All the scholars, though they differ as to detail, agree in placing "Julius Cæsar," "Hamlet," "Othello," "Macbeth," "King Lear" in the first decade of the seventeenth century, and in sandwiching between these masterpieces the atrocious plays of "Troilus and Cressida," "Measure for Measure," "Timon of Athens," and "Pericles." Is there another example of a very great artist who did his best and his worst work during the same decade? I do not know how to explain the matter, except by imagining that Shakespeare's instinct in the choice of tragic themes was unreliable. That he was in a tragic mood during the period in question is indubitable; but it seems to have been an accident with him whether he hit upon a theme that was suitable to his genius or not. If he happened to choose a bad theme, it ruined his play; for he had no conventional dramatic practices with which to sustain the piece.

If we have regard merely to Shakespeare's literary vehicle, we can see that his verse, his language and turns of thought, his metaphors and his music, show a consistent development from the beginning to the end of his life. His speech bewrayeth him. His form of thought becomes ever more rapid and elliptical; and the critics have had recourse to metrical theories in their attempts to date the plays. But we have no clue to Shakespeare's progress in that art which makes him Shakespeare: his dramatic craft seems like a series of miracles done upon a background of chaos. This lack of conventions was part and parcel of Shakespeare's age. The Elizabethan stage was a field upon which poets tried experiments in playwriting. There was no school of drama. If a man failed, he tried something new. This system produced both the greatest and the worst dramas in the world, and apparently Shakespeare wrote both kinds almost simultaneously.

XIII

THE SONNETS

Education sets spectacles before men's eyes. Each one sees what his learning and his avocations have taught him to look for; and thus the landscape of life resolves itself into a map. No two of these maps are exactly alike: your architect, your farmer, a university man, a theological student, a bank clerk — it is the early training of each that colors the world for him. He is seldom aware of this; for a man no more sees his own education than a man can see his own spectacles. It is the same with the fine arts. What are they but metaphysical lenses, a mental table on which men arrange their thoughts and feelings, bending over their poem, their plot, their picture, till the task absorbs their mind, and the work of art they leave behind teaches us to see what they saw, feel what they felt, be what they were?

The amateurs, and those who dabble in poetry, philosophy, or painting, think that these arts are clever games, played with bits and fragments of experience. But to the artist and the poet the games are life itself. Their palettes and brushes, their majors and minors are parts of a harness which their souls have somehow slipped into, and by means of which their lives and experiences are mysteriously transmuted into poetry, plays, pictures, and so on.

Although no one knows how Shakespeare was employed between the ages of twenty and twenty-eight, when he emerged as an actor and dramatist, it would seem that the playhouse was his university. He was dipped in the theatrical business at so early an age that its conventions formed and controlled his thought. All the modern playwrights except Shakespeare have something else in their minds besides drama. They have opinions, prejudices, intentions — a training and a private life outside of their craft. If, for instance, a modern dramatist reads Aristotle's "Ethics," he thinks about Aristotle and about ethics; but if Shakespeare reads Aristotle's "Ethics," he sees both Aristotle and Ethics dancing in his mind as part of a puppet-show that never ends. In the flush of his youth he entered the Cavern of Drama, where is enacted the eternal mystery play of human life. None of the creatures of the mystery play are persons, but resonances, realms of feeling, diapasons of the spirit. They are musical antiphonies which, when sounded properly, evoke that unity within us which responds only to the counter-strokes of mighty opposites.

Young Shakespeare stepped into this cavern and was never heard of again. The stage became his education; the drama was his life. We are puzzled by this — we who have been taught to see life as politics, religion, or morality; as conduct, or economics. We insist that there must have been some part of Shakespeare that we could meet outside his playhouse; and we almost resent the fact that he has no private opinions, and ask petulantly, "What did the man do for the rest of the day after his playwriting was finished?" Well, he staged-managed a theatre, acted in plays, and went to the tavern to meet his friends. That is all that we positively know about him. Between the cavern and the tavern Shakespeare was content. He belonged to that class of artists who live for their work, like Mozart, Turner, Rembrandt, or Blake; and as his work was from the start very much appreciated, and he was, moreover, of a most happy disposition, he had no temptation to fume and worry, to wonder whether it was good, to struggle and suffer and write letters, and in one way or another to expose his own relation to his art. If he had any feelings about himself and his work, he worked them off, as he did the rest of his thoughts, in depicting stage characters.

That Shakespeare excited so little notice while he lived, and left so few personal records behind him, is indeed puzzling; but then we have no one with whom to compare him. Perhaps men like Shakespeare always live and die unnoticed. If a single specimen of a new insect should be found, and if its chrysalis should turn into a butterfly leaving no shell behind, we should be astonished at the rarity of the species; but we should not cry out that the absorption of the shell was a miracle. Shakespeare's mental grasp, facility, and learning so amaze us that he seems like a creature from another planet; and yet we are forced to judge him by our own. His dramas throw no direct light on his life; nor do the two romantic poems, "Venus and Adonis" and "Lucrece," for these poems are obviously pieces of formal art. Therefore the famished curiosity of the world has fixed itself upon his Sonnets.

A convention of heavy-footed critics, with shovels on their shoulders and cans of dynamite at their elbows, have been encamped about Shakespeare's Sonnets for a century. They feel that they are about to excavate Shakespeare, and set him up definitively in their museum. They think that, if they but knew the facts of his life, and the identity of W. H., to whom the Sonnets are dedicated, they would pluck out the heart of his mystery and write their names on his tomb. But the mystery of the Sonnets is a mystery that can be delved into only by imaginative perceptions which are apt to be blunted by learning. The study of documents hurts the eyesight.

The sonnet-form is a humorous opal, which hides or discloses its lights according to the sky and the weather, and turns to trash in a museum. It has a history that is knitted into the social life of Europe for six centuries; and the customs and costumes of Italy, France, and England are reflected in its hues. It forms a class of literature by itself: for the sonnet is not written to be printed, but to be shown in manuscript to one's friends as a social amenity. To publish sonnets is a pompous and academic thing to do, and is like handing about dead butterflies in a box. Petrarch established the practice, and thereby did much harm to the art. Shakespeare's Sonnets were not meant to be printed, and are thus true and lively creatures. Neither were they holy and intimate confessions, consigned to the drawers of a secret cabinet and found after his death by a friend. They were written from time to time during three years, and at a period when a sonnet-craze reigned among the literati of England, having been brought in from France in the wake of Renaissance influences.

The sonnet throughout its history had remained a highly specialized type of literary performance, conventional, candied, and dealing with conceits which had become common property. The vast authority of Petrarch controlled its form and substance for two centuries before Shakespeare's time, and the Elizabethan sonnets are imitative to a degree that was unsuspected till the scholars exposed the facts. What would have been thought plagiarism and theft in any other form of poetry was deemed correctness in the sonnet. The whole art and craft of sonnet-making was governed by ideas of the supersensuous which are vaguely attributed to the influence of Plato. The verses lived in a planetary region, above the touch of earthly passion, and the women to whom sonnets were written became metaphysical stalking-horses for the poets. Dante was not in love with Beatrice in any ordinary sense of the word, nor Petrarch with Laura, nor was Sir Philip Sidney in love with Stella. The feudal worship of imaginary womanhood mingled in the sonnet with a metaphysic of beauty and a cult of virtue.

There is, however, a difference between the Elizabethan sonnets and their continental forerunners which has not been sufficiently noticed by the scholars. The language of the continental sonneteers was more archaic than that of their British followers. In old Italian and old French sonnets the roses are wired upon an idiom which explains the pose and foundation of the whole art. Had Shakespeare adopted the Italian form of the sonnet, or used an archaic or mannered vehicle, as Dante does in his "Vita Nuova" or Ronsard in his Sequences, the difficulty of interpreting his Sonnets would vanish. We should accept them as things of exotic beauty, impersonal and symbolic, which derive their immortality from the intellect and make appeal to the intellect. But Shakespeare's Sonnets are written in the most ruddy, fluent, spontaneous, inspired vernacular that the English language can show. Their frequent anticlimaxes, their constant carelessness, their monotonies, their absurdities, are sustained and floated on a lyrical genius of the first order. There is no poetry in the world quite like them. Shakespeare thus turned the sonnet into something it had never been before; for its ideas and conceits remain absolutely impersonal and supersensuous, while its language has become warm, rippling, and offhand.

It is wonderful that the single bit of Elizabethan gossip that has come down to us should give us what we most want to know about Shakespeare's Sonnets, namely, "how they struck a contemporary." In 1598 Francis Meres, in reviewing current poetry, wrote that "the sweet and witty soul of Ovid lives in mellifluous and honey-tongued Shakespeare, witness his 'Venus and Adonis,' his 'Lucrece' and his sugred sonnets among his private friends." Sugar'd sonnets among his private friends! I doubt whether anything has ever been said about Shakespeare's Sonnets that explains them better than these six words. Open them anywhere, and lines or phrases of such rapturous felicity greet us that we seem to hear the wren.

> Mark how one string, sweet husband to another,
> Strikes each in each by mutual ordering;
> Resembling sire and child and happy mother,

Who all in one, one pleasing note do sing.

. . . .

When forty summers shall besiege thy brow,

. . . .

Shall I compare thee to a summer's day?

. . . .

When to the sessions of sweet silent thought, . . .

The Sonnets should be dipped into, or read by the half-hour together, singly or in sequences, and without any special effort to understand them; for they have been written in a mood of quietude and relaxation, perhaps the gentlest mood that the gentlest poet ever knew.

In reading them to-day, we are under certain disabilities due to our own age. During the Renaissance the passion for beauty and for the looks of things led men to rediscover the fact that very great beauty merges into something that is a symbol, a divine thing, intellectual, and, as it were, superhuman. The chairs and tables and portraits and palaces of the Renaissance have this splendor for the eye. The Italian and French literatures of the period are steeped in a passion for objects, for statues, processions, pictures, personal beauty. This passion invaded England and attacked the poets. Spenser was its most eminent victim, but Shakespeare by no means escaped. His "Venus and Adonis" and his "Lucrece" are plastic, beauty-maddened, Italianate performances — pagan if you like, and a part of that pagan period which produced the supreme animal perfection and godlike unmorality of Titian's portraits. Sheer beauty was felt as a power, a dynamo, an intoxicating influence.

The symbolic, impersonal quality of all the Cinquecento work is the inimitable part of it. Modern painters and poets are forever expressing their intimate personal feelings; and we have had during the last century such a downpour of the personal in the work of Byron, Wordsworth, and Keats; of Tennyson, Browning, Mrs. Browning, Musset, Heine, and the rest, that our very conception of a poet is of a man who writes a private journal in verse, who hugs himself and sings. He uses ideas and abstractions merely as a means of expressing his private feelings and personal experiences. But the Cinquecento school made use of its private feelings and personal experiences to express abstract ideas. You will say that the matter is of small importance, so long as something beautiful is produced in either case. But the matter is important from the point of view of autobiography. For instance: if you credit Tennyson with having felt toward a particular man the sentiments which he expresses in "In Memoriam" for Arthur Hallam, you do right. But if you credit Shakespeare with truly feeling toward a particular man the sentiments which he expresses in the Sonnets for his patron, you do wrong.

Tennyson is undoubtedly laying open his private feelings; for such is the poet's ideal in Tennyson's age. Shakespeare is expressing a mood which he understands, has felt, when or how we know not — perhaps only in that heaven of invention where he found Romeo, Imogen, and King Lear. The Shakespeare of the Sonnets is merely one of Shakespeare's characters, and he sprang out of the book and volume of Shakespeare's brain, — out of all the trivial, fond records that youth and observation copied there, — even as Romeo, Imogen, or King Lear sprang from the same source. And this personage of the Sonnets disappeared — just as Romeo, Imogen, and King Lear disappeared — with the occasion that gave each of them birth. Just what the circumstances were that gave rise to the Sonnets we do not know; but even if we knew all their details, we should still have to understand them by a light which we are apt to forget — the light of The Sonnet.

Shakespeare's Sonnets were almost certainly paid for by his patron, and were certainly handed about freely among the wits of the time. To our taste it seems absurd that Shakespeare should have written seventeen sonnets to a young nobleman, beseeching the lad to beget children in order that his beauty might be transmitted to posterity. But we must remember that the exchange of absurd sonnets was a social game, lately introduced from France, which everyone was playing when Shakespeare wrote. I can go as far as believing that the pampered boy was handsome, and perhaps resembled a portrait of Adonis by Giorgione; but I cannot believe that Shakespeare was sincerely anxious about the continuance of the human species by this youth. If it were the case of Tennyson, I should believe every word the poet said. I should be surprised, of course, that any man should have strong feelings about such a matter; but I should accept Tennyson's word for it. In the case of Shakespeare, however, I feel that what the sociologists call the "play-instinct" is involved. To speak brutally, it is a joke.

The first seventeen Sonnets, when viewed in this

light, thus explain their artificiality as perfectly as if Shakespeare had written them in an archaic language. The extraordinary beauty of certain lines in them fails to raise in our minds any problems as to Shakespeare's biography: we accept the lines as poetry. And indeed the Twelfth Sonnet is one of the most beautiful that Shakespeare ever wrote: —

When I do count the clock that tells the time,
And see the brave day sunk in hideous night;
When I behold the violet past prime,
And sable curls all silver'd o'er with white;
When lofty trees I see barren of leaves,
Which erst from heat did canopy the herd,
And summer's green all girded up in sheaves,
Borne on the bier with white and bristly beard;
Then of thy beauty do I question make,
That thou among the wastes of time must go,
Since sweets and beauties do themselves forsake,
And die as fast as they see others grow;
    And nothing 'gainst Time's scythe can make defence
    Save breed, to brave him when he takes thee hence.

Now it is natural to suppose that Shakespeare, having discovered a new talent in himself in writing the first seventeen Sonnets, proceeded to write many more in the same manner. The order in which they are printed is not quite authoritative, for they are supposed to have been published piratically by the booksellers. The general theme of them is the celebration of ideal love — precisely the theme of Dante and of Petrarch. The mood they depict is not the mood of one who is in love, but the mood of one who knows what love is. There is a monotony about the theme, as Shakespeare himself several times points out; yet he manages to draw music out of the repetitions.

I confess that, if these Sonnets were all that had been left by an unknown poet of Elizabeth's age, I might have been deceived into regarding them in the modern light as confessions. I might have asked the question put by Richard Grant White: "Would Shakespeare, or the man for whom he wrote, have shown about among his friends these evidences of so profound an emotion, these witnesses of an intellectual struggle that went near to shatter his whole being?" But when I think of the pictures of passion *in women* that Shakespeare has left us, of Juliet, of Venus, of Rosalind, of Cleopatra, — pictures which certainly do not represent personal episodes and which owe their power to the fact that they are purely imaginative, — I cannot help classing the Sonnets in the same list. Such poetry as is in Shakespeare's Sonnets is not the record of any particular passion: —

> The poet's eye, in a fine frenzy rolling,
> Doth glance from heaven to earth, from earth to heaven;
> And, as imagination bodies forth
> The forms of things unknown, the poet's pen
> Turns them to shapes, and gives to airy nothing
> A local habitation, and a name.
> Such tricks hath strong imagination,
> That, if it would but apprehend some joy,
> It comprehends some bringer of that joy.

The biographical value of the Sonnets is that they show how slight was the occasion out of which Shakespeare, through his passion for abstractions, was able to draw those pictures of love-in-absence, lovers' quarrels, love at unequal ages, love's forgivenesses, love's happiness, which have been the comfort of lovers of both sexes ever since.

Let us turn over the pages of the Sonnets and observe that, whenever one of them is so whimsical or so defective that it keeps us alive to the playful or half-playful nature of the whole series, we do not torment ourselves with biographical interpretations of it. We cannot, for instance, believe that Shakespeare lay awake at night, or at least for *many* nights, thinking about the beloved youth; or that he felt himself to be in hell when separated from the young swell. We cannot believe that Sonnet Number 42, in which the poet forgives the idol for having seduced his own mistress, represents a soulful revelation; or that the very beautiful Sonnet Number 95, in which the poet forgives the idol for being a thoroughly bad lot, is the utterance of personal passion. Both numbers 42 and 95 belong to a whole class of gentle, passionless, deprecatory sonnets, written on the theme, "Upon thy side against myself I'll fight." This idea is a philosophic abstraction of the first water, and could have been arrived at only by a mind which had passed through passion and was living in the beyond. Each of these gentle sonnets is a toy of the brain made to express the abstraction. But it is a toy like the mariner's needle, with which the whole of earth and all the heavens are in conspiracy. A current of gigantic power is running through these toys. Shakespeare himself, though he knows they are toys, does not know they are powerful. He thinks he is merely giving to airy nothings a local habitation and a name. But, for my part, I have seen so many good minds destroyed by opposing the current in these sonnets that I shall use a pointer, move rapidly, and attempt no cataloguing or digest of their meanings. I shall content myself with throwing out a guess or two in the direction of their general nature.

I will first quote one in which the thought is so quizzically expressed that we perceive it to be *sheer thought;* and yet it is so true a picture of what happens in the mind of anyone who is in love, that one can see how passion flashes out of it for the lover.

43

When most I wink, then do mine eyes best see,
For all the day they view things unrespected;
But when I sleep, in dreams they look on thee,
And, darkly bright, are bright in dark directed.
Then thou, whose shadow shadows doth make bright,
How would thy shadow's form form happy show
To the clear day with thy much clearer light,
When to unseeing eyes thy shade shines so!
How would, I say, mine eyes be blessed made
By looking on thee in the living day,
When in dead night thy fair imperfect shade
Through heavy sleep on sightless eyes doth stay?
All days are nights to see till I see thee,
And nights bright days when dreams do show thee me.

So also Number 31 shows the consecration that love — I mean *being-in-love* — casts upon all our previous emotions. This Sonnet would perhaps mean little to one who had not been in love — yet it catches and expresses one of the subtlest of life's experiences.

31

Thy bosom is endeared with all hearts,
Which I by lacking have supposed dead;
And there reigns love, and all love's loving parts,
And all those friends which I thought buried.
How many a holy and obsequious tear
Hath dear religious love stol'n from mine eye,
As interest of the dead, which now appear
But things remov'd, that hidden in thee lie!
Thou art the grave where buried love doth live,
Hung with the trophies of my lovers gone,
Who all their parts of me to thee did give:
That due of many now is thine alone:
Their images I lov'd I view in thee,
And thou, all they, hast all the all of me.

Of the same import is Number 53, which I quote because of its affectation and carelessness. It is a queer sonnet, it is cruelly artificial; but the idea it contains is as profound as Plato, and more truly expressed by Shakespeare than by Plato; for Shakespeare does not dogmatize, but leaves the thought in the vague where it belongs.

53

What is your substance, whereof are you made,
That millions of strange shadows on you tend?
Since every one hath, every one, one shade,
And you, but one, can every shadow lend.
Describe Adonis, and the counterfeit
Is poorly imitated after you;
On Helen's cheek all art of beauty set,
And you in Grecian tires are painted new:
Speak of the spring and foison of the year,
The one doth shadow of your beauty show,
The other as your bounty doth appear;

And you in every blessed shape we know.
In all external grace you have some part,
But you like none, none you, for constant heart.

The Sonnet last quoted gives the heart and kernel of an idea that Plato elaborated somewhat ponderously in his "Symposium." I will confess *en passant* that some of the Sonnets are incomprehensible, because the thought has become too attenuated — for example, Numbers 67 and 68; and that one or two of them are disgusting — for example, Number 118. But all are baubles, and this symbolic quality is the only quality they all have in common.

In those that I have quoted thus far the element of paradox and *jeu d'esprit* is apparent; but when you come to the very great sonnets, where the poetic part is perfectly expressed and the idea is obvious, and represents a universal experience, it is almost impossible, while reading one of them, to keep one's head. We could almost swear that the poet is in love. Let the reader glance through Number 98.

98

From you I have been absent in the spring,
When proud-pied April, dress'd in all his trim,
Hath put a spirit of youth in everything,
That heavy Saturn laugh'd and leap'd with him.
Yet nor the lays of birds, nor the sweet smell
Of different flowers in odour and in hue,
Could make me any summer's story tell,
Or from their proud lap pluck them where they grew;
Nor did I wonder at the lily's white,
Nor praise the deep vermilion in the rose;
They were but sweet, but figures of delight,
Drawn after you, you pattern of all those.

Yet seem'd it winter still, and, you away,
As with your shadow I with these did play.

76

Why is my verse so barren of new pride,
So far from variation or quick change?
Why with the time do I not glance aside
To new-found methods and to compounds strange?
Why write I still all one, ever the same,
And keep invention in a noted weed,
That every word doth almost tell my name,
Showing their birth and where they did proceed?
O, know, sweet love, I always write of you,
And you and love are still my argument;
So, all my best is dressing old words new,
Spending again what is already spent:
For as the sun is daily new and old,
So is my love still telling what is told.

52

So am I as the rich, whose blessed key
Can bring him to his sweet up-lockèd treasure,
The which he will not every hour survey,
For blunting the fine point of seldom pleasure.
Therefore are feasts so solemn and so rare,
Since seldom coming, in the long year set,
Like stones of worth, they thinly placed are,
Or captain jewels in the carcanet.
So is the time that keeps you as my chest,
Or as the wardrobe which the robe doth hide,
To make some special instant special-blest
By new unfolding his imprison'd pride.
Blessed are you, whose worthiness gives scope,
Being had, to triumph, being lack'd, to hope.

I have chosen these favorites almost at random; and the point I would make — also a paradox — is that it is because Shakespeare's best sonnets are completely intellectual and dispassionate, that they make so personal an appeal. They are, after all, no more convincing than "Hamlet." Our own most inner chords can be made to vibrate, whether through music, architecture, or poetry, only by forces which have passed through some prism or crystal of the mind, and which are as impersonal as geometry.

The fact that these Sonnets were addressed to a young man has distressed the critics of the after-world; though it is to be observed that the masses of mankind have always accepted them simply, each reader taking his share of them as poetry. There exists, of course, such a thing as love between persons of the same sex. This kind of love is often true and noble, and contains an element of passion. It has been hymned by Milton in his "Lycidas," by Keats in his "Adonais" and by Tennyson in his "In Memoriam." This sort of love is apt to run into extravagances and vices, and is a troublesome kind of passion. An attachment of this sort may possibly have had some share in the creation of Shakespeare's Sonnets. I do not see it there myself. I see only reminiscences of ordinary love evoked by fancy, expressed in terms of passing fashion, and controlled by the mind of the greatest poet that ever lived.

If Shakespeare had given us in his Sonnets pictures of lust and debauchery, I should still not regard them as throwing much light on his personal history, for they would have been as ideal as his Tarquin. He eludes us in the Sonnets as completely as in the plays, and for the same reason: his mind had the power of grasping abstractions that are larger than we can compass. We are led to suspect that a brain such as his *could* not evolve the personal; he translated it into an abstraction as soon as he saw it. In the process of expressing a private opinion, he turned it into a generality, and this habit became so inveterate with him, and he became so alarmingly clever, so completely absorbed in the explosions of his thought at each moment, that we are shaken and surprised, as perhaps he was; but it is only the universal in ourselves which is touched. It is the impersonal, the divine, that we get from him, whether in play or sonnet. We find our own intimate thoughts in him, and exclaim, as Stephano did when he heard the music of the invisible Ariel, "This is the tune of our catch played by the picture of nobody."

APPENDIX I

NOTE ON ENUNCIATION

In all great art there seems to be a lightness of touch, a transparency, a fluidity attained without loss of weight — as if a thing could be at the same time both a mountain and a mirage. This supersubtlety of the vehicle itself daunts the beholder, or overcomes him like a summer cloud. We do not know how the thing is done, or on what it depends. When we read poetry to ourselves, there is nothing between our minds and the mind of the poet; the vehicle is purely intellectual; the ideas of the poet pass from his mind to ours in silence. But when poetry is read aloud, recited, or acted on a stage, new arts come into existence, the arts of speech and gesture, and the like, and the new arts must partake of all the power and all the subtlety of the verse behind them.

Though it is impossible to decide how much of charm a good delivery can lend to verse, it is plain that a bad delivery will destroy any poetry whatever. In the plays of Shakespeare almost every idea is syllabled by someone on the stage. Stage directions are rare. If there is a knocking, the porter says, "Knock, knock, knock"; a modern playwright would have relied on a stage direction. But on Shakespeare's stage every character is, like Prospero, surrounded by Ariels, to whom he talks in asides. They all soliloquize. Soliloquy, the bugbear of modern dramatists, is Shakespeare's main reliance.

When an actor who has been trained in the modern drama plays Shakespeare, he is apt to make either too much or too little of his lines. The school he has learned in is a school of crude simplicity, of long pauses and dynamic effects, of melodrama rubbed in by heavy psychology. The flashes and cadenzas of Shakespeare, his leaps into the beyond and sudden turns of humor and extravagance, outrun the modern stage. Your actor, perhaps, tries to dramatize his lines and relate them to his conception of the part. Alas! he must first have a conception of the poet himself. The nimble-footed naturalism of Shakespeare demands a Proteus who can turn at will into air, fire, or water, into Puck, Mercutio, or Malvolio.

A Shakespearean play is a headlong race of wit, pathos, and expressiveness. The actors must vibrate like musical instruments, and shake off a thousand fancies with facility, while their major passions are rumbling underneath and uncoiling at the proper time.

In the acting of poetic drama every effect is connected with *enunciation* — with the lips, teeth, tongue, voice, and intonation of the actor. This part of his performance must be absolutely perfect, and with a perfection that merges into the action and beauty of the rest and becomes lost in the thoughts behind his words. The speech of an actor, his whispers or his roars, must be modulated and edged with a delivery as delicate as the sting of the bee; for this enunciation, even when it seems to be lost on the ear, qualifies his whole rendering and gives it a refinement which nothing else can give. The following is Dr. Doran's account of Edmund Kean as Sir Giles Overreach, the miser, money-lender, and extortioner in Massinger's play, "A New Way to Pay Old Debts." I cite the passage as a tribute to the power of elocution.

"In this last character, all the qualities of Kean's voice came out to wonderful purpose, especially in the scene where Lovel asks him, —

> Are you not moved with the sad imprecations
> And curses of whole families, made wretched
> By your sinister practices? —

to which Sir Giles replies: —

Yes, as rocks are
When foamy billows split themselves against
Their flinty ribs; or as the moon is moved
When wolves, with hunger pined, howl at her brightness.

"I seem still to hear the words and the voice [of Edmund Kean] as I pen this passage; now composed, now grand as the foaming billows; so flute-like on the word 'moon,' creating a scene with the sound; and anon sharp, harsh, fierce in the last line, with a look upward from those matchless eyes, that rendered the troop visible, and their howl perceptible to the ear; the whole serenity of the man, and the solidity of his temper, being illustrated less by the assurance in the succeeding words than by the exquisite music in the tone with which he uttered the word 'brightness.'"

Perfection of utterance is the basis of acting. It is an artificial accomplishment, attained by study and developed by practice. We enjoy good recitation when we hear it, but we have forgotten that it is an art. In the matter of painting or music, we quite concede that any good work — anything that counts as art — is the result of accurate knowledge. We know that the orient which shines about any finished production is the outcome of lifelong study and of a grind over detail. The grind has been continued for years, and about it there has hung little suggestion of clouds or of beauty, but rather the dust and chips of a workshop.

In the matter of singing, the professionals have educated our public. No one thinks that good singing is a gift of the gods, or that a child will sing well by nature. But in the matter of speech the American Educator of to-day is prone to set the little darlings on the stage and let nature be their teacher. Their beautiful souls will instruct them. Let them make their exits and entrances; let them recite their lines, and do their business according to the impulse of their pure little hearts; and we shall, no doubt, have such acting as can never be attained by instruction. The results of this sentimentalism are seen in our children's performances. Behind the sentimentalism, nevertheless, and obscured by it, there lies a truth, which the musical world knows well, and which the theatrical world will discover as soon as it takes up the training of children seriously. The performance of a talented child who has received a thorough grounding in technique has in it a divine element, a grace of its own, an impersonal, seraphic charm, which one cannot expect from the grown-up artist, and which is one of the æsthetic mysteries of the world. In the matter of acting, child-talent is common — it is very common: it is much the commonest of all artistic talents — but it is as helpless before a play as a musical child would be if confronted with a church organ. The child's hands must be placed on the keys and its mind adjusted to the music. It must be taught.

If you will take the pains to train a set of children averaging, say, eight years old, to play the "Tempest," or some smaller play, which is expressed in language far above their comprehension but which deals with ideas that are entirely within it, you will find that the children at first have to be taught every speech and gesture. They do not know what the whole thing is about. They recite like little monkeys, and take each speech by itself. The words and gestures which they learn teach them the idea — in scraps and at moments. They do the work before they understand the doctrine. As the day of dress-rehearsal approaches, however, the children begin to see the life of the story behind its separate scenes; and note this: it is the story that they see, rather than their own several parts in it. They have not an isolated "conception" of their own rôles, but a general conception of the whole plot and its progress, and of their cues as part of the story.

To endeavor to give a child a conception of his part is to confuse him. Let him act the part, and his conception will be the outcome — not a thought, but a dramatic exhibition. As a rule, this understanding of what the whole play is about falls like a climax upon a company of children after a month of hard work; and they do wonders.

The special beauty and pathos of children's work is due to two elements: the ingenuousness of their natures and the *finish* of their performance.

The moment the detail becomes slovenly, the charm vanishes. This is so apt to occur in children's plays that perhaps one should regard it as a normal feature of them. When the children have once made a success, and feel self-confident, they are apt to get excited, to forget their careful diction, and carry all before them with enthusiasm and fine acting.

On the instant that they do this, the beauty drops out of the show, and the educator must recur to first principles and give the urchins further drill in accurate speech and formal stage behavior.

I take it that grown-up actors might learn something useful to themselves by observing how children best attain a true relation to their rôles: it is by never thinking of the rôle as a separate problem. The "conception" of a part, the conception of a part! I will not say that a Shakespearean actor who is drenched in the whole atmosphere of the plays can do himself much harm by working up a conception of Othello or Romeo. The elder school of actors got their training as children do, and were master-craftsmen in recitation and in stage behavior before they were old enough to lay claim to an important rôle. But a young actor, or a new Shakespearean, had better never think of his rôle as a separate thing, but follow the thought of the author and of the audience, which is always fixed on the thread of the story.

I doubt very much whether Shakespeare himself had any "conception" of his separate characters. And why should one go to building up a set of phantasmal conceptions, and then letting them loose in a situation which is already complex enough without them? We see these so-called conceptions battling and cutting each others throats in amateur theatricals, where there is often room for nothing else but them upon the stage. It is hard work and self-effacement that counts in the end.

APPENDIX II

AMERICAN SPEECH

In America, education occupies the attention of everyone; and this is one of the most hopeful things that can be said about our outlook. We are beginning to wonder what education is, and what part of it is connected with schoolbooks.

There has, within the last generation, grown up a scattered class of enthusiasts who are interested in speech. It was revealed to them, perhaps by some deep semi-religious instinct, — one of those impulses by which Nature saves herself, — that a person who could *articulate* was a civilized being. They discovered, as it were by a miracle, that the brain, the heart, the attention, the muscular system, the soul and body, were drawn to a focus in the act of speech, and that education began here.

Perhaps, also, the danger that threatened our language through the influx of foreigners, and which was reflected in the speech of our own children and of their intimates, frightened these new prophets. Perhaps the suspicion passed through their minds that, unless they bestirred themselves, they would soon not understand the lingo that was being spoken in their own neighborhood.

Certain it is that many minds among us have been awakened to the importance of articulate speech. This is a matter that has never been neglected in Europe, where people have always taught their children to speak carefully, as a matter of course, and in the same spirit in which they put a spoon in the hands of a baby who is old enough to feed itself.

But the effort to improve our speech in America must be self-conscious and dogmatic; because a large part of our population believes that babies will find spoons for themselves, and that good speech comes by nature, and is at best a foolish thing.

The problem of reforming the speech of America would seem ghastly and hopeless, but for the fact that such a reform is mimetic rather than rational. Many a man has reformed his own speech in middle life through contact with someone whose voice and utterance he admired. His ears became sharpened.

As for the young, they need only a model and good-will to show a change for the better in a week. Give a shock to a certain portion of their consciousness, and they become aware of their own deficiencies: they hear their own horrors: the rest is easy. There will, no doubt, be many dogmas, many methods, and every one of them will act as a stimulus and a step in advance. When our people shall have come to understand the importance of Articulate Speech, the first province of Learning will have been conquered.

It makes little difference what pronunciation is adopted, so long as the vocalization is good. The Scotch utterance is to my mind beautiful, and reveals the remarkable intellect of that people as clearly as anything they have accomplished. Should America develop a pronunciation totally different from the British pronunciation, there would be nothing to regret so long as it was good.

But if you slur and gargle your mother-tongue, I question whether your mother-wit will ever do much for literature. The voice is so much a part of the brain, that you can hardly think clearly and yet speak in gibberish: and this is the great and wonderful discovery that America is making.

The bearing of it on Shakespeare is obvious enough; for the reading of him comes in the wake of seeing him acted, seeing him acted in the wake of reading him, and both come as the strongest stimulus the world has ever known in the provinces of speech and of thought.

APPENDIX

A Shakespearean troupe is a traveling university, with this advantage over other universities that it reaches the young. It inculcates good speech by example, and in the very moment that it does this, it points to the place where true education should begin, — has always begun, — namely, with the study of the great poets.

McGRATH-SHERRILL PRESS
BOSTON